WAR IS NOT ALL HELL

THE STORY OF COMRADERIE
AND FRIENDSHIP BORN IN TIMES OF WAR

William R. Covington

iUniverse, Inc.
New York   Bloomington

WAR IS NOT ALL HELL
The Story of Comraderie and Friendship Born in Times of War

Copyright © 2010 William R. Covington

All rights reserved. No part of this book may be used or reproduced by any means, graphic, electronic, or mechanical, including photocopying, recording, taping or by any information storage retrieval system without the written permission of the publisher except in the case of brief quotations embodied in critical articles and reviews.

iUniverse books may be ordered through booksellers or by contacting:

iUniverse
1663 Liberty Drive
Bloomington, IN 47403
www.iuniverse.com
1-800-Authors (1-800-288-4677)

Because of the dynamic nature of the Internet, any Web addresses or links contained in this book may have changed since publication and may no longer be valid. The views expressed in this work are solely those of the author and do not necessarily reflect the views of the publisher, and the publisher hereby disclaims any responsibility for them.

ISBN: 978-1-4502-3352-1 (pbk)
ISBN: 978-1-4502-3353-8 (ebook)

Printed in the United States of America

iUniverse rev. date: 7/19/10

ACKNOWLEDGEMENTS

I dedicate this book to my three children, Britt, Cindy and Currie and their spouses, Sherry, Brian, and Mary Leigh, and to my grandchildren, David, Cameron, Holden, Avery, Campbell, Larson, Parker, Cooper and Ansley. They have brought more joy and happiness into my life than they could ever have imagined. May God continue to bless them all.

    I would also like to dedicate the book to those that have served and are currently serving in our military forces, and especially to those comrades in arms who paid the full measure. To be sure, our many freedoms, our opportunities, and our safe living environment in the USA did not and do not come without a price.

CONTENTS

Acknowledgements v

My Inspiration ix

CHAPTER ONE

Fall, 1962 - March, 1965 Flight Training 1

CHAPTER TWO

April, 1965 - June, 1965 Ft. Wolters, Texas 23

CHAPTER THREE

July, 1965 Deployment From San Antonio, Texas 31

CHAPTER FOUR

August, 1965 1st Tour – South Vietnam 39

CHAPTER FIVE

September, 1966 – December, 1967 Ft. Benning, Georgia 79

CHAPTER SIX

January, 1968 – July, 1968 Ft. Sam Houston, Texas 87

CHAPTER SEVEN

July, 1968 – July, 1969 2nd Tour – South Vietnam 91

Conclusion 131

Tributes, Acknowledgements, and Other Thoughts 133

About the Author 135

MY INSPIRATION

This is a story of one individual, and a number of the people, places and very meaningful events that have proven to be extremely monumental in the author's life and his desire to make a difference, at least in his own mind.

CHAPTER ONE

FALL, 1962 - MARCH, 1965

FLIGHT TRAINING

Well, it's time to write this book. Why? I'm currently 68 years old and realize that I have many more yesterdays than I do tomorrows. More importantly, I promised my three children and myself that I would do it so they could be a bit more aware and understanding of me and a period of my life that they actually know very little about. The fact is, that during the period covered in the book, my youngest son, Currie, was not born and my other son, Britt, and daughter, Cindy, were very young.

Another reason is that I want to share with my friends, comrades and any others that have had similar experiences. I hope to shed a bit of a different light on the subject of war with an emphasis on the humor that often happens during such times. I truly believe that such humor is one of the major factors that assist in getting one through such times in one's life experiences. I have truly cherished this period of my life and know that it had a great deal to do with developing the positive attributes of my character that I may have and the way I have approached and lived my life.

As an ROTC graduate from Wake Forest University, I entered the U.S. Army as a Second Lieutenant, Medical Service Corps. I completed the MSC Officer Basic Course at Ft. Sam Houston, Texas in the fall of 1962 and was assigned as the Headquarter Unit Commander, 85th Evacuation Hospital, Ft. Chaffee, Arkansas.

In January, 1963, my wife Jenny, and my nine-month old son, Michael Britt, joined me at Ft. Chaffee. I had told my wife that we would be seeing a lot of the world during what I intended to be a two-year tour of duty in the Army.

As I remember, after approximately six months in the Ft. Chaffee area, Jenny asked me if this assignment was my idea of 'seeing a lot of the world'. Even though I liked my job, my Unit, my Commander and the Arkansans that I had met, I had to admit that there just wasn't much to see in the immediate area.

Even though we had planned to serve only two years in the military, we agreed that I would apply for some type of school that would give us a geographical change. In an effort to increase my chances of being selected for a school, I decided to apply for both airborne and flight training. After submitting my applications, it occurred to me that in my youth, it actually frightened me to climb up on our carport which was all of twelve feet high. Oh well, such is life.

In order to apply for flight training, one had to pass a flight physical which required 20/20 vision (uncorrected) with no color vision problems. You also had to pass an aptitude test which was heavily oriented toward flying. Once I passed these two requirements, I was scheduled for a helicopter orientation ride. Though I was never told, I believe that this requirement was to determine if I had a fear of flying. Since I had flown a total of only two times in my life, once as a passenger in a single-engine Cessna and once in a commercial aircraft to San Antonio, Texas, I was confident that the orientation flight would be no problem. I was told that a helicopter would be arriving and to meet the pilot at the nine hole Ft. Chaffee golf course.

I was excited, since this would be my first ride in a helicopter. The flight in the OH13 lasted about 15 minutes, seemingly with no unusual maneuvers to determine whether or not I had any fear of flying. In a few months, I received orders to attend Fixed Wing Flight Training at Ft. Rucker, Alabama. The assigned class was to begin in February, 1964.

ARRIVAL AT FORT RUCKER

Upon arrival at Ft. Rucker, it quickly became apparent to me that the Army was in the initial phase of a large aviator build-up in support of some type of conflict outside the USA. I was told that there was a good possibility, due to the large number of trainees already in school, that there would be a delay for me and others to begin our training.

I could write an entire book about flight training and other related experiences at Ft. Rucker and Ft. Wolters, but I will only dedicate a portion of this book to those experiences. You may wonder why I, as a Medical Services Corps Officer, received a quota for the Officer Fixed Wing Course instead of the Rotary Wing Course. So did I. The fact is, the vast majority of the aircraft assigned to the Army Medical Services Corps are helicopters, not fixed wing aircraft. I can only surmise that during this period, the fixed wing quotas were more available and once one became a graduate, the two month Rotary Wing Qualification Course could immediately follow.

As I expected, I initially became what was known as a 'snowbird', meaning that I would be waiting for a slot to open in a fixed wing class in order to begin my training. As a snowbird, I was assigned to one of the Support Divisions with a Major Smith as my supervisor. He had become aware that I had attended Wake Forest University on a baseball scholarship and informed me that I would be the Special Projects Officer (SPO) to coordinate and supervise the construction of a number of Little League baseball fields on the main post area. During this snowbird period, we completed three of those fields, all of which my son Britt (a two-year old at the time), would later play some of his youth baseball. I would also like to add that I was Britt's coach during those times.

FLIGHT TRAINING

In a few months, I was assigned a class and date, 64/7 in my case. At our initial orientation briefing, I remember very distinctly that the speaker stated that no more than 70% of us would graduate. In our particular case, it turned out to be around 65% percent. A few were set back to a previous class and eventually graduated.

The speaker's comment on the expected dropout rate was a bit discouraging, but he did make a more positive comment. He said, "Those of you that do graduate will join the ranks as a proud Army aviator." That comment made me feel better and a bit more determined to graduate.

In 1964, Fixed Wing Flight Training was divided into three phases: A) Primary; B) Tactics; and C) Instruments. I will never forget my first day of 'A' phase at Shell Field in Enterprise, Alabama. The instructors were all civilians and appeared to be between 40 and 60 years old. My instructor, Mr. Sheffield, seemed to be one of the younger ones. A fairly large number of them had some scars, facial wrinkles, and appeared to be quite a bit older than their actual age would indicate.

I remember saying to one of my stick buddies, "Do you think this is how we might look after a career in aviation?" He laughed. Now, after realizing what we, as students, put those instructors through, I can certainly understand their outward appearances.

Mr. Sheffield was a sincere, thorough, and meticulous type of instructor. I recall that on my initial dual flight in the L-19 Birddog, Mr. Sheffield instructed me to take the controls and follow him through a couple of take-offs and landings. I actually felt like I was flying the aircraft. So much for the good part. After a few landings and takeoffs, he said that we would go out to the upper air work area and he would demonstrate some maneuvers such as turns, stalls, spins, etc. that I would be required to perform at a later date. I felt that I was doing fairly well until we did a stall, followed by a spin, with recovery. I had been on the controls during the normal turns and stalls, but when the spin started, I immediately turned loose of the controls, took my feet off the rudders and grabbed the upper supports in the ceiling of the cockpit.

Soon thereafter, Mr. Sheffield, in strong tone via the aircraft intercom, said, "Lieutenant, stay on the controls during these maneuvers." I got back on the controls and followed him through the recovery procedure. I must admit that soon after another spin recovery procedure, I became nauseated and threw up in the cockpit. Upon landing, and after hosing down and cleaning the aircraft, I slowly began walking to the flight debriefing room where Mr. Sheffield would be waiting. I was concerned that I was about to be booted from the program or at least, put on probation. Upon arrival at the briefing room, Mr. Sheffield said two things to me, both of which I have never forgotten.

He said, "Lieutenant, go to the hospital, explain what happened, and request some medication that does not preclude flying and will insure that you never throw up in my aircraft again." Then he said, "You appear to have a good attitude. Keep it, and you have a good chance of becoming an Army aviator."

To this day, I have never forgotten his remarks about attitude, regardless of the difficulties that I have encountered both in life and in my aviation career. I took the medication until it ran out and was never nauseated again during 'A' phase. Mr. Sheffield was pleased and so was I.

'A' PHASE

'A' phase was the period geared toward learning the basics of flying. We would spend half of the day in the classroom being taught such things as flight characteristics, aircraft maintenance, navigation, meteorology, radio procedures, map reading and other similar basic subjects associated with flying. The remainder of the day would be spent flying the L-19 Birddog. Our initial hurdle as students was to learn to take off and land the aircraft without the instructor being in the aircraft. The term used was 'soloing'. The average time for this to be accomplished was between 10-12 hours of flying experience. Even though we, as students, had taken off and landed the L-19 a number of times without our instructor's assistance, it was still a big deal to actually accomplish the task by ourselves. Such things as "What if the engine fails or some other emergency happens?" all would creep into our minds.

As I remember, I soloed at around the eleven hour mark. I also remember that one of my friends and classmates was the first to solo well before the ten hour mark. He appeared to be what we others thought of as being a 'natural'. I must admit that my friend became a bit cocky after being the first to solo. But as the saying goes, "Every dog has his day."

After a number of additional flight hours, both dual and solo, we were required to demonstrate our ability to perform three types of landings. The three were a power on spot landing, a front wheels only landing, and a power off spot landing. All solo. The rule on the power off spot landing was that once you cut your power on downwind or base leg, you were not allowed to add power again. Your flaps setting was optional. We were all told that during our individual landings, our instructor would be monitoring from the airfield tower with binoculars.

So how did "Mr. First to Solo" do on this requirement? He added too much flaps on the power off spot landing, either on base leg or final approach, and was going to be short of his spot. He had to add power, resulting in a pink slip (failure) for the requirement. As I remember, it took 'flaps' (his well-deserved nickname) three more attempts to pass this requirement. He was really downhearted but we all kept encouraging him and he bounced back quickly.

Another interesting, but sad thing, happened during 'A' phase. One of my section mates, Joe, who was doing real well both academically and flight wise, called me one night and said, "You don't have to pick me up for flying tomorrow morning." I didn't think much about it until Joe didn't show for training the next couple of days. I later learned that he had voluntarily dropped out of training. One of the reasons that this surprised me was that Joe was usually the one who would ask the flight and/or the academic instructor some type of intelligent question and he always appeared to be one of the most dedicated students in our class. Normally, most of us felt that it was best to keep our mouths shut so as to not show our ignorance. Those of us that knew Joe fairly well were saddened that he quit, regardless of the reason. As time progressed, we learned to cope with eliminations and hoped that we would not be the next one to go.

Let me relate one more story concerning soloing. Early on in training, it was quite easy to characterize certain types of individuals. There were a small number that came over as a bit cocky and in our sections case, one individual seemed to standout. Now, far be it for me to instigate any kind of devious action, but when that particular classmate soloed, I thought it would be appropriate to celebrate his success in some type of special way. It was mutually decided by me and some of my close buddies that we would throw said individual off a particular bridge in Ft. Rucker on our way back from Shell Field. I made our bus driver aware of our intentions and he agreed to stop the bus at the particular bridge for the celebration. I must admit that 'Ranger' Reilly put up a good fight, but our numbers prevailed.

A few days after the celebration, we were all instructed that such a celebration would not happen again due to the fact that the particular creek was snake-infested and that someone could be severely injured. Someone spoke up and said, "Hell, he's a Ranger and snakes have been known to die after biting a Ranger". Reilly even laughed at the statement.

I would be remiss if I didn't relate my first, but not my last, failure (pink slip) during flight training. My friend 'Flaps' wasn't the only one to have a bit of a problem successfully accomplishing the power off spot landing during our 'A' phase training. I had a similar problem but decided to handle the situation a bit differently. I had nailed both the power on spot and the front wheels only landing, but on the power off spot landing I, too, had reduced power a bit early. Feeling that I could still make the spot, I came up just a little short of the hard surface runway. When I hit the ground, red dirt and dust flew everywhere as I simultaneously applied power to become airborne. If there was a transmission from the tower to me, I either did not hear it or unconsciously ignored it.

Upon completion of the three landings, we had been instructed to depart Shell Field and go practice solo upper air work. Since the airfield tower personnel were quite busy with numerous aircraft at the time, I thought that just maybe Mr. Sheffield, having seen me complete the first two landings successfully, had already left the tower to take care of some other paperwork.

Not too long after arriving at the upper air work training area, I received a call to return to Shell Field and report to my instructor. To say the least, I was both ashamed of attempting to get away with the short landing and also concerned that I might be booted from the program. When I entered the student briefing room, a number of my classmates began applauding my arrival. This really confused me. Walking toward my table, I immediately made eye contact with Mr. Sheffield. In his hand, he was holding a pink slip. When I sat down, he looked me in the eye and said three things: 1) Poor judgment; 2) The power/throttle is your friend; and 3) Let's see how you do tomorrow.

Now, I don't know about you, but when Mr. Sheffield gave me what I knew was a tremendous break, I decided at that time that I would work extremely hard to be the best student that I could possibly be. To this day, and especially during my family life and military career, I have felt that no one is perfect and more times than not, if you give someone a break, they will turn out better and be more effective than they were before.

'B' PHASE

Upon completion of 'A' phase, we would now engage in what was to be a much more diversified and fun phase of flight training. 'B' phase would consist of learning flying techniques used in a tactical environment. We would be expected to learn flying skills well beyond the ones taught in 'A' phase. Such skills as confined area work, barrier, approaches and takeoffs, and road landings would be taught. We would certainly use the basic skills of flying taught in 'A' phase, but 'B' phase was not only going to test our flying skills, but was going to develop and test our judgment under difficult circumstances. We would also do a fair amount of night, tactical flying which was always exciting in a single-engine aircraft.

A former dentist and now Army aviator named Captain Dodds would be my 'B' phase instructor. Early on, he informed me that he would be teaching me certain skills that would make flying more natural and less mechanical. I looked forward to that type of training. Even though I knew that I was well-coordinated in certain sports, having played football, baseball and basketball for a large portion of my life, I was still not real comfortable flying an airplane.

Many exciting and interesting things happened to me and my classmates during 'B' phase training. I will save the best and happiest ones for later, just to hold your interest.

Early on, we were informed that we would be flying out of a stage field just north of our base, Lowe Field. We would learn to pick up ground messages with an attached aircraft lanyard with a hook. We would also practice barrier landings and takeoffs. The plan called for the instructor to demonstrate these skills dual, then we were expected to perform them solo. I remember being so excited on my initial solo barrier takeoff that I accidentally keyed my radio mike. This resulted in my inadvertently transmitting the verbal instruction I had previously received from my instructor on our dual barrier takeoff to the ground radio operator and classmates in the area. It went something like this.

"Brakes, flaps, full power, rudder control, stick back, clear obstacle/barrier, reduce flaps, reduce power, correct for crosswind", and then I verbally congratulated myself with a, "What a perfect takeoff, Blue 63", which was my call sign.

Suddenly the ground radio operator transmitted, "Blue 63, check mike." Naturally I felt like a fool and took a lot of ribbing back at the student briefing room.

Let me go ahead and relate another embarrassing story before we move on to some other exciting moments in my training career. Our section was scheduled to complete our night solo cross-country. The flight would consist of three legs and if flown properly, we would arrive back at Lowe Field with an adequate amount of fuel in reserve. I calculated the winds, the distance to be flown at an altitude of 2500 feet, and figured the reserve fuel to be right at thirty minutes.

So far, so good. I made the first leg right on time, but was a couple of minutes late reporting completion of the second leg. I figured, no problem, there must be a slight wind change. The night was quite dark with no moon and a bit hazy as I remember. Well, for whatever reason, I was not seeing my third leg checkpoints. After what seemed like a long time to me, I felt that I was quite a bit off my intended course back to Lowe Field. I haven't mentioned this yet, but unlike Rotary Wing students, we were issued parachutes in case we encountered an in-flight emergency requiring exiting the aircraft.

At this time, I was not in the panic mode but I must admit that I was rapidly becoming a bit concerned about my situation. I tightened my parachute leg straps and decided to climb to a higher altitude in hopes of seeing some familiar site such as Dothan or Ft. Rucker.

At an altitude of 4000 feet, and heading north, I saw a white, rotating beacon. We had been taught that if you became a bit disoriented/lost, you could use what was called a DF Steer. This simply meant that you could key your radio transmitting mike and the receiving tower/radio personnel could locate you and give you a heading to your desired destination. I implemented this procedure with my home base, Lowe Field, I was given a compass heading and directed to proceed directly to the airfield for landing. Shortly before reaching Lowe Field, I was asked by the tower operator to state my location. I replied that I saw an airfield to my right front.

The tower operator replied, "Blue 63, that's Cairnes Army Airfield. Do you know where you are now?"

I replied, "Yes" and was both embarrassed but thankful that even if I ran out of gas at that moment, due to my altitude I had a choice of either Cairns or Lowe for my power off night landing.

Two things happened after I landed and taxied to the parking ramp at Lowe Field. At the student briefing room, my instructor informed me that there had been a major wind change from a southerly wind to a northerly wind and that a number of students had sought assistance. Even though that made me feel a bit better, I still received a lot of harassment from many of my classmates. Such harassment came with the territory and was expected.

Another flying exercise for our section was to depart Lowe Field at night and proceed to a stage field approximately fifteen minutes southeast of Cairnes Army Airfield for some short strip takeoffs and landings. The stage field had a number of parallel strips that would accommodate two separate traffic patterns operating simultaneously. The majority of our L-19 training aircraft were olive green but as it happened that night, two white aircraft had been assigned to students, one of them being me.

When I arrived at the stage field, there were already quite a few aircraft in both flight patterns doing landings and takeoffs. After my first landing and takeoff, I heard the tower operator speaking with a student who seemed to be quite disoriented. He was having a problem entering his designated traffic pattern. As I was making my second landing, the disoriented student flew over the approach end of both pattern's landing runways at quite a low altitude. I, like everyone else, was naturally concerned about a possible mid-air accident.

While on the ground, I again monitored the tower operator giving pattern entry and landing instructions to the disoriented student. I was cleared for departure for another takeoff and landing which would complete my three stage field landings.

On downwind and shortly before turning on base leg, I again heard the tower operator, this time in an excited voice, instruct the confused trainee to exit the area and return to Lowe Field. In my effort to locate the position of the confused student, I failed to monitor my altitude indicator. That wasn't good. On my turn from base leg to final approach, I was so low that my left landing gear struck the ground. I immediately added power and flew by the tower at about 100-150 feet. As I was climbing out to exit the traffic pattern, I used my flashlight to check my left landing gear which appeared to be just fine. The tower operator requested for the white aircraft that had landed short to identify itself. I attempted to do so a couple of times, but was interrupted by radio traffic from other aircraft. By this time, I had exited the stage field traffic pattern and was well on my way to Lowe Field.

After landing at Lowe, I checked and verified that my landing gear was fine. Fortunately, there were at least two other white aircraft assigned for the exercise. I was never asked again by anyone with authority if I had been the one who hit short of the landing strip, and I wasn't about to confess. I could only figure that due to the fact that the stage field was not closed for landings due to the confused student, no one wanted any further investigation into the situation. It was determined later that the disoriented student was in fact night colorblind and could not distinguish runway lights from taxiway lights. He was immediately eliminated from the flight program.

Continuing with some of my night flying adventures, I would like to share another story that turned out to be a bit interesting.

As a part of our tactics training, our section was scheduled to bivouac at one of the stage fields west of Enterprise, Alabama. Flying out of that area, we would accomplish some more of our tactical requirements, one of which was a dual pilot, night cross country. On this particular mission, we would be required to identify and report certain checkpoints.

By this time in the training program, I had become good friends with Lt. Garnett Crask, a former ROTC graduate from the University of Kentucky. The flight scenario was a bit like my solo night cross country, except over different geographical terrain. We both felt that being a dual flight, this cross country would be a piece of cake.

All went well, with our first and second leg turn reports over designated checkpoints being right on time. The problem occurred as we approached our bivouac stage field for landing. We monitored over our radio that due to large number aircraft waiting for landing clearance, aircraft were being stacked at different altitudes. About five minutes from the stage field, we called for landing instructions. We made several more attempts, but received no reply from the tower operator. Not knowing exactly what to do upon arrival at the stage field and receiving no communication from the tower operator, we decided that we would enter the traffic pattern and land. We transmitted our intentions 'in the blind', blinked our landing light a couple of times, entered downwind in front of another aircraft, and landed.

After landing, we taxied to the refueling point, refueled and proceeded to the parking area. We filled out our aircraft log book and noted that our radio/receiver was inoperative. We then went to our two-man pup tent for what we thought was going to be a good night's sleep.

It wasn't too long after all the aircraft noise had subsided that we heard a voice shout, "Crask, Covington, are you in the tent?"

We responded, "Yes, sir."

He continued to state that he was very pissed off with us and that he had personally performed a ramp check to verify that our aircraft was in the parking area and that we were safe.

He then asked, "Why didn't you contact the tower for landing and logging in?"

We both simultaneously responded, "We tried, sir, but our radio was inop."

He responded, "Lieutenants, I'm going to personally check your radio and you better pray that it doesn't work."

Since we didn't get another visit, we figured that he couldn't get the radio to work either. We later learned that our visitor that night was none other than the Major in charge of our tactical training.

That particular night was quite cold for South Alabama and while asleep in our two-man pup tent, I unintentionally attempted to snuggle up to Garnett, my tent mate. It was cold, and I was obviously trying to get a bit warmer. I was immediately awakened with an elbow to the ribs and a, "What are you doing?" Once again, I was asleep, and that's the truth.

We all successfully completed our training at the stage field in a couple of days and returned to Lowe Field.

One of the fun traditions during 'B' phase was for you and your instructor to fly down to DeFuniak Springs, Florida and have some of the best pizza in that part of the country. Well, not too long after my first trip, some of my friends and I decided that since we had enjoyed the pizza so much, why not meet back there on one of our solo flight periods?

By this time in our training, those of us that were left were allowed to fly solo and practice the tactics that we had been taught. This idea to go to DeFuniak Springs really caught on because on certain occasions, the parking ramp there was full and you would have to wait for someone to leave.

It wasn't too long before our active duty flight leader stated that a call had been received from the pizza place asking why only students were showing up for pizza? He then stated such visits were supposed to be dual only. Naturally, no one confessed such an understanding.

At about this point or even earlier, I'm sure a large number of you are wondering just how we got away with so many borderline actions. Without going into a lot of detail, I will simply say the army was a bit different during those times and add that I'm so thankful to have been a part of it.

'B' phase was not just about flying. We also had academics and other requirements, one of which was the 'escape and evasion' course. What I am about to relate is by no means a recommendation to any future or present student in any type of school, military or otherwise. I will just relate the story as it actually happened.

In the classroom, we were taught methods and techniques of survival and escape, depending on the situation. To me, it all boiled down to the fact that one should do whatever is required to survive or escape when confronted with the possibility of dying or being captured.

After receiving our escape and evasion classroom instruction, we were shown the map area of where we would begin the course, the boundaries, and the completion point. There would be aggressors throughout the area, and those captured would be duly treated. The distance to be covered would be approximately seven miles with terrain consisting of thick wooded areas and streams. One of the last remarks by the classroom instructor was, "Don't get captured."

The exercise would be conducted during darkness. We would travel in twos and as it happened, I was paired with an Iranian student named

George Gaffari. In the next few days, some of my classmates and I discussed our upcoming requirement/adventure and many ideas were tossed around as to how we could complete the requirement without being captured.

I, and some others, will never forget that one of our classmates stated that he had personally reconned some of the area and found a cornfield where we might secure some corn to eat along the way. Actually, raw corn didn't appeal too much to me, so I will just leave it at that.

A couple of other classmates that had been paired with Iranians approached me and we all decided that evading during the night through tough terrain would be very difficult with an Iranian that spoke and understood very little English. That being said, the three of us along with our three Iranians decided on another method of completing the course. Our plan was to enter the escape and evasion zone, remain there for a designated amount of time, then rendezvous at a specific area to be picked up later by a friend.

Once we were picked up, we would then go to a safe area, remain there for awhile, then be transported to an area west of the objective. At an appropriate time, we would arrive at the objective. The Iranians were overjoyed and excited about such a plan and we all agreed that it had to be kept secret.

A couple of interesting things happened during this actual exercise. One of my classmates and his partner had decided to do the same thing as us. But on their way to their pickup point, while trying to escape, he was captured. He was also injured when he ran into some barbed wire. Later on, he relayed to me that while being transported to the Ft. Rucker hospital to receive some stitches in his leg, he was behind our pickup vehicle, recognized me, and was very tempted to have the ambulance driver turn on his rotating lights and siren to scare the hell out of us. Thank God, he didn't.

Having not actually gone through the entire escape and evasion course, you may be wondering how we appeared upon arriving at the final destination point to report in to the cadre. Well, we all rolled in a ditch prior to our arrival to make sure we appeared a bit worn out from the nights travel. It worked. Looking back, our actions were not the most noble nor the right thing to do, but at the time, I think it was. Again, do I recommend such an action? No.

'B' phase was fun and exciting and gave one a realistic view of Army Fixed Wing Flying. It also provided an atmosphere where one could develop some lasting friendships. At the end of the phase, one of my most cherished memories happened.

My wife, Jenny was pregnant with our second child. On the very day that she went into labor and I took her to the hospital to deliver, I was scheduled for my final 'B' phase check ride.

When we arrived at the hospital, and after Jenny had been seen by a doctor, I was told that it would be quite a while before delivery. I was told to go ahead and take my check ride and then return to the hospital. To say that my nervousness and excitement levels were high would be a tremendous understatement. By the time I reached the flightline, the word had already spread that I had taken my wife to the hospital to have a baby. My check pilot, Captain Chancelor, asked how my wife was doing.

I think I said something like, "As well as can be expected."

He said, "Relax, and let's go have some fun flying!"

That statement did relax me and I really appreciated his attitude. To this day, I don't remember all the requirements he had me complete but the check ride was fun and certainly seemed to progress rapidly.

When we landed, he said, "Covington, go to the hospital to see your wife and new baby." He also said that I did fine on the check ride. I had now completed 'B' phase.

Upon arrival at the hospital, I was told that I could join my wife in the pre-delivery room. When I arrived, I found Jenny in a much different mood than Captain Chancelor. I won't mention any details about the language and/or details of what she said to me. Just suffice it to say, after escaping her grasping hand, I told the nurse that I would get out of the way and wait in the waiting room. That experience taught me that women in labor are normally not their nice, normal self.

Not long afterwards, the nurse came to the waiting room with our new child wrapped in a blanket. Expecting another son, due to the fact that both my mom's and dad's families were predominantly boys, I was about to be surprised.

The nurse said, "Want to see your new daughter?"

My response was, "No, it's a little boy."

The nurse simply said, "Why don't you take a look?"

I did, and for sure, our Cindy was a beautiful, little girl and a true blessing to our lives. By the way, not too long ago, I informed Cindy that her birthplace at Ft. Rucker, once a WWII cantonment-type hospital, is now filled with pine trees.

To celebrate the completion of 'B' phase, the class decided to have an afternoon beer bust at the Ft. Rucker Lake Lodge at Lake Tholocco. You can imagine how happy everyone was to be two-thirds of the way toward becoming Army Aviators.

Many of us had become really close friends and a great deal of comraderie and pride was very obvious. We had continued to lose some classmates to attrition and/or being set back to a trailing class. Though we regretted that fact, we all knew that we had to bear down in order to complete our 'C' phase instrument training.

Due to our past flying episodes (good and bad), a number of nicknames or 'handles' were used to identify us. Some that I remember were Tiger (Clemson Tiger Mascot) Lloyd, Hoot (old movie cowboy) Gibson, Owl (big eyes) Tracey, Ollie (Laurel & Hardy) Becker, Brandy (drinking and smoking habit) Brandcamp, Flaps (excessive use thereof) Ipock, Buzz (not sure here) Sawyer, and last, but by no means least, Ranger (graduate of Ranger School) Reilly. I was simply called Cov.

Remember Ranger Reilly as the target of the bridge tossing incident? Well, much to my surprise, Ranger Reilly had not forgotten that episode. And obviously someone along the way had spilled the beans that I had been instrumental in his creek emersion.

About halfway through the party and standing not too far from the water's edge drinking my beer, I was attacked from behind with what I would describe as a Ranger strangle hold. Before I knew it, I was in the water and felt that drowning was a distinct possibility. I'm not exactly sure just who or how many came to my rescue, but to this day, I am very thankful for their help. The episode evolved into a number of other friendly lake tossings. As for Ranger Reilly and myself, we continued to be good friends, both feeling that justice had been served.

The afternoon beer bust went so very well that we decided a class dinner party would be nice before we began our 'C' phase training. It was quickly planned and would also take place at the Lake Lodge. Remember our escape and evasion course and the fact that I was paired with one of the Iranian students named George Gaffari? He and I had become good friends. Since wives and girlfriends would be invited to the dinner party, George asked me if I knew anyone that could be his date. It's been quite awhile since flight school, but I think I got George a date with a lady from Ozark, Alabama that I had either worked with or met during my 'snowbird' time.

Well, after George, my wife and I picked up George's date and were on our way to the party, I heard a bit of commotion coming from the backseat of my car. Initially, I didn't pay much attention but shortly thereafter, my wife said to me, "Billy, do something about what's going on in the backseat." Looking in to the rear view mirror, I saw that George was being a bit aggressive.

In a stern voice, I said, "George, behave and cut that out." He cooperated and at the party I let George know that such actions were not accepted by Alabama ladies and especially on the first date. He smiled and said he understood.

The party was great and enjoyed by all. We were now in a great frame of mind to move on to what might be our most difficult phase of training.

'C' PHASE

The word was that in 'C' phase, we would lose or have set back twice as many classmates as in either 'A' or 'B' phase. Naturally, that concerned us all, but also made us aware of just how important it was to learn instrument flying. That very fact came back to me in some extremely sad cases during my aviation career.

We would be required to learn to fly a different aircraft, the U6 Beaver. But the major emphasis was to learn instrument flying and not contact flying. We would be using a hood (preventing outside viewing) and/or actually flying in weather conditions.

To me, the actual weather flying without the hood was much easier, and I welcomed those days. One of the main reasons I felt that way was because you could not only watch your cockpit instruments better, but you could observe exactly what your instructor was up to as far as pulling circuit breakers, etc.

My initial 'C' phase instructor was Caption Cavanaugh. He was large in stature, a former college football player, a combat arms type, and a rated Mohawk Pilot. Even though he never exemplified the fact, I always felt that he had much rather been instructing in the Mohawk Transition Course than in the 'C' phase flying the single-engine Beaver.

One of the requirements in starting the Beaver was to prime the engine with fuel. The primer knob was to the left and below the bottom of the left cockpit student seat. Often, due to the fact that I would initially raise my seat and buckle my safety straps, I would have a problem reaching the knob to prime the engine.

After a couple such occasions, Captain Cavanaugh would say, "Mrs. Covington, having a problem priming the Beaver?"

Always being embarrassed since there were at least one or two stickmates in the back of the aircraft monitoring the conversation, I quickly adjusted to give myself the leverage to properly prime the engine before starting.

Regardless of the ribbing, I liked and respected Captain Cavanaugh. I also never relayed the story about the time I tackled and broke the ankle of a 200-pound high school fullback from Greenwood, South Carolina. That incident occurred during a football scholarship tryout to attend Wofford University. At the time, I weighed 135 pounds and no, I wasn't offered a scholarship, but later received a baseball scholarship to Wake Forest University.

Not more than two to three weeks into instrument training, Captain Cavanaugh received re-assignment orders and my stickmates and I received another instructor, a civilian named Mr. McCary. He was quite different from Captain Cavanaugh and I was pleased to have him as my new instructor. Some years later, I returned to Ft. Rucker for the Fixed Wing Twin Engine Transition Course and flew with Mr. McCary, only this time on a checkride. He was a great instructor and man.

It was not uncommon in 'C' phase for an instructor change for a student that showed potential, but was having a bit of a problem. My best friend, Garnett Crask, got the 'short end of the stick' on such an occasion. He had previously told me that his instructor, Lt. Anderson, was great and that he was doing well. A student switch occurred and Garnett had to move to a new instructor. After only one flight, Garnett informed me that his new instructor was pure hell in the cockpit and that he was a bit worried. A few flights later, Garnett stated that the instructor hadn't changed a bit, but fortunately his two stickmates were having more problems than he was.

Both Garnett and I passed our initial C1 checkrides and decided to go to Panama City Beach for the weekend to celebrate. We convinced our wives that it would be best if we did this as a bachelor weekend. At the beach, we did the things that one would expect out of a couple of young, flight school students. We went to some clubs, drank more than we should have, and overall had a great time. During Saturday, the weather deteriorated and it began to rain, which lasted all day and into the night. Having more drinks than we should have, we both got rain soaked that Saturday night and didn't get to bed until the wee hours of Sunday morning.

Probably as a result of this 'bachelor weekend', I contracted pneumonia and was put in the Ft. Rucker Hospital for five days. Upon returning to the flight line, I was informed by our Flight Leader that I was going to be set back to the class following us. Naturally, I wanted no part of that and requested to be allowed to fly extra periods in order to catch up so I could graduate with my classmates. In order to do this, I would have to miss some of the classroom instruction, but still take the required tests. Fortunately, we had finished most of the classroom work so I figured this would not be a problem.

Realizing how much it meant to each of us students to graduate with our beginning classmates, the Flight Leader got my request approved. A major was assigned as my instructor and I would be his only student. Two lessons were learned by me, at least for awhile. One being that celebration is good, but excessive drinking is not. Secondly, what may seem like a bad break, can sometimes turn into a good one.

The major and I seemed to hit it off and my instrument flying training went well. As for the academics, some of my buddies gave me a bit of tutoring help and I passed the remaining test with no problems.

Getting to fly double periods was really an advantage in a number of ways. I was able to quickly catch up, and actually got some extra training. The major was happy because instead of doing office work, he was getting to fly. It was easy to see that was what he liked.

On one occasion, I think that I was introduced to what one could call 'an unanticipated event'. We were under actual instrument conditions on radar at 5,000 feet and just chewing the fat. All of a sudden the engine sputtered and quit. I was flying the aircraft at the time and was about to initiate engine failure procedures when I saw the major reach for the fuel tank selector handle. He simultaneously reported to ATC (Air Traffic Control) that we would be momentarily out of 5,000 feet and would call back. The engine immediately restarted and I climbed back to 5,000 feet. The major reported to ATC that we were back at our assigned altitude and on course. We continued our conversation and nothing was said about the incident at my post flight debrief. Being as smart as I am, I surmised that I would also keep it to myself.

After receiving what the major felt like was adequate instrument flight training, he said, "I'm putting you up tomorrow for your final 'C' phase flight check."

I simply said, "I'm ready."

The next day, I passed the checkride and thankfully would be graduating with my class.

Our original class was right at 100 students. There were 63 of us at graduation, 10 of which were setback students from a previous class. We were 52 'originals', and were very proud to become Army Aviators. Naturally, my wife, Jenny, our son, Britt, and our daughter, Cindy, attended my graduation, but I was also thrilled and appreciative that my 'B' phase instructor, Captain Dobbs, came to congratulate me.

The majority of graduates would be assigned to fixed wing units. A few would be going to single or twin-engine transition, such as Mohawk, U8, or Caribou, prior to reporting to their assigned units. Roger Hula and I, both Medical Service Corps Officers, would be going to the two-month Officer Rotary Wing Qualification Course at Ft. Wolters, Texas prior to our unit assignment.

CHAPTER TWO

APRIL, 1965 - JUNE, 1965

FT. WOLTERS, TEXAS

It was decided that my family (my wife, son, and daughter) would stay in Rockingham, North Carolina, our hometown, while I attended the Helicopter Qualification Course at Ft. Wolters. In case you don't know, Ft. Wolters is located about 50 miles west of Ft. Worth, Texas. I was excited and felt confident about completing the course with no problem. All of the instructors were Southern Airways civilian contract personnel and the average age was a bit younger than the contract 'A' phase flight instructors at Ft. Rucker.

My instructor was a pleasant, low-key type individual that said, "William, my job is to teach you to safely fly the Hiller OH23D helicopter and your job is to learn this without breaking the aircraft or any of the flying rules while you are here for the next two months."

I felt good about the fact that he congratulated me on recently becoming an Army Aviator and he also stated that we would have some fun during the helicopter training. The atmosphere was quite different from Ft. Rucker in that failure was never mentioned.

I would like to mention a point or two about my perspective on learning to fly a fixed wing aircraft as compared to a helicopter, especially one like the OH23D with a manual throttle. If you are familiar with fixed wing flying, you know that you basically have two rudder (foot) control pedals, and a stick or yoke to control the ailerons. You also have a lever/throttle to control the amount of fuel/power that is needed for flight. You basically have two feet and two hands to operate these four requirements.

The OH23D helicopter is similar, except for one very important aspect. In this helicopter, instead of a throttle, you have what is called a collective pitch/power control operated by your left hand. Not only can you add or decrease pitch/angle to the main rotary blades, you must always adjust the amount of power/fuel needed. So both feet have a job in changing the pitch in the tail rotor blade. The right hand controls the cyclic/stick to maneuver the main rotor mast. The left hand manually controls both the pitch/angle in the main rotor blades and the fuel required for the flight maneuver. So when hovering or flying the OH23D, you have five requirements compared to the four required for fixed wing flight.

After three to four hours of flight instruction and not being able to successfully hover the aircraft, I told my instructor that the helicopter was not made to hover. He smiled and said, "All will come together in due time."

I was in total disbelief at this particular time of my training. A few flight hours later, and during hovering practice, I glanced over at my instructor and was totally surprised that he was sitting back in the seat with his arms folded instead of assisting me. Immediately, the aircraft started to waddle a bit, but as I turned my head to the front, the aircraft stabilized and he said, "Relax, you have the controls."

Now, if you were to ask me how one learns to hover a helicopter, I would say, "At a certain point, it just happens."

The interesting thing about it is that once you get it, you seem to never lose the technique. I would also relate, having been both a fixed and rotary wing aviator, that after any substantial absence from both type aircraft, normally one can transition back to the rotary wing more quickly than to the fixed wing.

The day after I hovered by myself, my instructor and I flew a short, dual period. After an approach and landing, he instructed me to hover over to a vacant area and land the OH23. I figured that we were going to do some more hovering practice, but he unbuckled his safety harness, looked at me and said, "Take it around a couple of times and come back and pick me up."

I thought to myself, "He is my instructor, so he must be confident that I am ready to solo."

I was excited, but felt that he knew what he was doing. My traffic patterns went fine and I began to feel that I was becoming 'a real helicopter pilot'. Boy, did I have a lot more to learn.

After soloing, we continued to practice dual autorotations, always to the ground. After my first one, it actually became fun. We learned to land on pinnacles, do side hill landings, do numerous power off forced landings, and lots of confined area landings and takeoffs. During these flight periods, I really became impressed with the capabilities of the helicopter and really enjoyed my flying.

We did both our dual and solo night training, including a night solo cross country. On this night solo cross country, I learned just how much a sizable crosswind can affect a small helicopter in maintaining a direct route to one's destination. Suffice it to say, I didn't have a lot of fuel remaining when I arrived back at the Ft. Wolters heliport.

Due to the fact that all my classmates and I were all rated fixed wing aviators, the failure rate was extremely low for the Rotary Wing Q Course. This fact was quite different from Ft. Rucker, where we lost so many of our classmates.

Upon graduation and without my family, I proceeded directly to Ft. Sam Houston to join my assigned unit, the 498th Air Ambulance Company. The 498th was commanded by Colonel Joe Madrano, a commander that I would grow to both respect and become very fond of during my time in the unit and afterwards. I also learned a great deal from Colonel Joe.

The 498th was a newly formed unit with 25 new UH1D Bell helicopters. My eyes truly lit up when I saw the first one. Both First Lieutenant Hula, my classmate in both the fixed and rotary wing courses, and I were welcomed into the unit. We were told that we would begin our checkouts in the UH1D and that the unit was preparing for an assignment to Southeast Asia. It was suggested that I leave my family in Rockingham, North Carolina since we would be deploying shortly.

We were told that we would be getting our UH1D checkouts with a 1LT Sylvester, a recently returning MSC Pilot from South Vietnam. This sounded good to me since I figured that 1LT Sylvester must have quite a bit of experience in combat flying. I was to learn shortly that I was correct in my assumption. I was given a copy of the Operator's Manual/-10 and told to read it and rely on the aircraft crew chief and 1LT Sylvester to answer any questions that I might have. Due to the time restraints, that was my 'ground school'.

Realizing that time was short, 1LT Sylvester pushed Roger and me pretty hard and attempted to teach us that which he had learned while flying in Vietnam. He was an extremely good pilot and there is no doubt in my mind that he played a big part in any success that I had while flying my two years of aeromedical evacuation/Dustoff in South Vietnam.

After learning to fly the UH1D in a basic sort of way, 1LT Sylvester taught me how to do some low level, high-speed approaches to a pickup site. He stated that using the terrain as cover and moving fast would greatly reduce the chances of taking hits on entry into and out of an area. This made sense to me.

He further stated that one's ability to successfully stop and land the helicopter in the designated pickup site would dictate the speed of the low-level approach. Point was, the better you were at stopping the aircraft without damage and without overflying the pickup site, the faster you could approach.

At first, never having done such maneuvers, I was a bit leery of the techniques involved. But as I progressed and experienced what Ernie Sylvester could do with the UH1D, I became more proficient and comfortable with the approaches. Soon I was able to carry my speed (90-100 kts) to a point just before the pickup site. Ernie always emphasized that you needed to stay as low as possible on the approach and to hover as little as possible in the pickup area. It was also important to keep the tail of the helicopter pointed toward any known enemy location, not only as a protective measure, but also to facilitate a rapid departure from the area.

Again, thanks to 1LT Ernie Sylvester, I felt that I had learned a great deal and would implement that which he taught me in my flying duties in Vietnam. Since Ernie did all or most of his first tour Vietnam flying in the III and IV Corps areas of South Vietnam (relatively flat terrain), it would not be until I arrived in the II Corps area of South Vietnam that I would need to develop a different type of approach. II Corps was more mountainous and sometimes required a rapid descent, high overhead, spiral approach to safely enter the designated pickup site. Here again, the idea was to use an approach method that would minimize exposure to enemy fire.

Back for a moment to my checkout with Ernie…

Toward the end of my checkout, Colonel Madrano, our Commander, said he would like to fly with me to see how my training was going. Though I felt honored, I must admit that I was a little nervous knowing that I would be flying with Colonel Joe who was a very experienced helicopter pilot. Later on, I learned that he had been an instructor pilot who was notorious for wearing black gloves and distributing numerous failure slips on checkrides. He became so known that 'The Black Hand' became his nickname, especially to those that feared his checkrides.

Our flight went well during the beginning when I was performing a series of standard maneuvers and approaches. Then Colonel Joe asked me to demonstrate some of the combat tactical techniques that 1LT

Sylvester had taught me during our time together. We were flying at a small, uncontrolled airfield just northeast of Fort Sam Houston and the terrain was quite flat with practically no obstacles. I said OK, and informed Colonel Joe that I would demonstrate a low level, high speed approach to a designated pickup point on the airfield.

In retrospect, he was probably expecting the low level approach to terminate with a decrease in ground speed well before the pickup point, with a straight forward flare, terminating at a hover, then landing. In order to make the approach as realistic as possible, I described the expected enemy situation, the entry and exit directions, and my plan to land with the tail of the aircraft pointed toward the enemy position.

Since the wind was calm, I stated that I should be able to avoid the enemy position on both entry and exit to the pickup site.

He simply said, "Sounds reasonable. Go ahead."

From 1000 feet AGL (above ground level), I lowered the collective/pitch and quickly got to treetop level approximately a quarter mile from the pickup point. My plan was to execute the aforementioned straight forward flare and land with my tail toward the enemy position.

All went well until I realized that the normal, straight flare was not going to enable me to stop the helicopter at the pickup point. I was going to be long – a no-no.

At that point, I remembered a technique that 1LT Sylvester had demonstrated that would additionally slow down the aircraft and I decided to use that technique. He had assured me that done property, there would be no undue stress placed on the aircraft frame or engine.

In order to stop the aircraft, I initiated the normal straight flare, coupled with a side flare and kick turn and landed the helicopter with the tail toward the reported enemy position. Once on the ground, I looked over at Colonel Joe, whose hands seemed to be coming down from above indicating that he had been holding on to something during the approach.

His disgruntled words to me were, "Sylvester taught you that?"

I said, "Yes, sir."

Needless to say, sometime afterwards, Ernie, with a bit of a smile, said to me, "Man, you got my ass in trouble with Colonel Joe."

To this day, when Ernie and I see each other, we both get a chuckle out of the incident. Again, I will say without any doubts, that this tactical flying which I initially learned from Ernie Sylvester saved me and my crews' tails on numerous occasions while evacuating patients in Vietnam. More to come about this fact later.

CHAPTER THREE

JULY, 1965

DEPLOYMENT FROM SAN ANTONIO, TEXAS

Kneeling L-R: Danhouser, Covington, Scharf, Price, Retzlaff, Bentley, Nash, Willcox, Jones, Beltran, Spruiell, Hula
Standing L-R: Haswell, Burroughs, Scott, Thackston, Rusiewicz, McBride, Madrano, Hopkins, Persons, Heinz, Mizell, Osborne, Mills
(Not in Photo: Rogers, Caroll)
498th AIR AMBULANCE COMPANY PILOTS
PRE-EMBARKATION 1965 – VIETNAM
COL. JOE MADRANO, CO

Not too long after my UH1D checkout, which amounted to 10 to 15 hours of actual flight time, we were alerted that we would be deploying to South Vietnam in a matter of weeks. We were also notified that we needed to fly a number of the helicopters to Mobile, Alabama in order to get them seaworthy for shipment on an aircraft carrier to Vietnam.

An interesting point about our 498th Air Ambulance Company was the officer rank distribution. As stated before, we were authorized 25 UH1Ds. Our officer deployment strength was twenty-seven MSCs (Medical Service Corps), which was approximately 50% of our authorized strength. We would deploy with one colonel, sixteen majors, six captains, and four lieutenants, me being one of the four lieutenants. As you can see, we were a bit heavy in field grade officers (major and above).

With many of the field grade officers busy getting the unit ready for deployment, it was decided that we would ferry the aircraft to Mobile single pilot, no crew chief, and in groups of four to five aircraft. With no names mentioned, my flight leader was an instrument examiner with lots of helicopter flight time and was either accompanied by another pilot or a crew chief. We were all on a VFR (Visual Flight Rules) flight plan and all went well until approximately fifty miles west of Mobile.

At 2,500 feet, the weather began to deteriorate with the ceiling falling rapidly. Suffice it to say, my flight was in a loose, staggered formation. At this point, I was in the third position from the flight leader with two other aircraft behind me. Suddenly, the two aircraft in front of me disappeared. Having been fixed wing instrument rated and having flown in the clouds during flight school, I maintained my altitude and lead, also flying into the clouds. My immediate thought was that I would soon break through, regaining VFR conditions.

I soon heard the two trailing pilots radio that they were IFR (Instrument Flight Rules) and breaking the formation for VFR conditions. In an effort to be as safe as possible in such a situation, I slowed the aircraft and stated that I would be descending on the east heading to also become VFR. I broke out of the clouds at 1,500 feet and radioed to the flight leader that I would be proceeding directly to Mobile. Fortunately, no one panicked and we all arrived at Mobile safely.

Discussing the incident later, and especially since we were flying single pilot, it was agreed that more forewarning could have been given by the flight leader in an effort to maintain VFR conditions. But, in such times, all is forgiven very quickly.

Shortly after returning from Mobile, I was informed that I was free to depart Ft. Sam Houston, Texas and join my family in Rockingham, North Carolina. I was told that I would be contacted with instructions on where to report for deployment to Vietnam. This was late June, 1965, and in mid-July, I received a telephone call instructing me to report to the naval yard in Savannah, Georgia to board the MSTS (Military Sea Transport Ship), the Upshur.

On the night of 12 July, I said goodbye to my wife, two children and some other family members and boarded a train for Savannah. I was very sad to be leaving my family and other loved ones, but was also very proud and excited to be going to a place where I knew that I could be directly involved in the saving of lives.

Keep in mind, this is July of 1965 and the real big buildup in South Vietnam was just beginning. Units were forming and being deployed at a very rapid pace. Since I was issued only a pair of one-piece flight suits and told that our other clothing and equipment would be issued upon arrival in Vietnam, I was travelling lightly.

I arrived at the Savannah train station the next morning and immediately secured a taxi to take me to the Upshur. The driver drove me to within fifty yards of what appeared to be an entry ramp to the ship. I paid him and in my civilian clothes, carrying my red, green and blue plaid suitcase, I walked to the ramp and spoke to a navy man who appeared to be in charge. The time was around 7:30 a.m. when I presented him with my military ID card. He then asked for my assignment orders and I informed him that I had not been issued any orders but was told telephonically to report to the Upshur for transport to Vietnam. By this time, a group of other ship personnel began to gather around me. I was asked what army unit I was assigned and I stated it was the 498th Air Ambulance Company.

At this time, he said, "Lieutenant, you have no orders, you are not in uniform, and I can't let you board this ship."

Thankfully he didn't mention my plaid suitcase. I was a bit tired from the train ride and beginning to get a bit pissed, and I think this was being noticed by one of the other ship personnel.

He stepped up and said, "Lieutenant, put on a uniform and we will let you board the ship."

I then informed him that all I had in my suitcase was a one-piece flight suit and where did he suggest I put it on.

He then said, "In about four hours, a band, lots of dignitaries and military brass are going to be here to welcome a large contingency of the 1st Air Calvary out of Ft. Benning, Georgia that will also be on the Upshur going to Vietnam."

He then said, "Go ahead and report to personnel at the top of the bridge for your quarters assignment and wear your flight suit when outside your quarters this afternoon."

I said, "No problem. Thanks."

At around 1230 hours, the band and dignitaries arrived, soon followed by the troops of the 1st Cav. The troops were in full combat gear, with weapons and were very impressive. I often wondered how I would have fared if I had arrived for ship boarding in my civilian clothes and plaid suitcase, simultaneously with the 1st Cav. Hell, I may have never made it to Vietnam, at least not on the Upshur.

Roger Hula, an MSC aviator like me, was assigned to bunk with two young Warrant Officer Aviators, both in the 1st Cav. WO1 Chip McCallister and WO1 George Rice had both just recently completed WO flight training. As I remember, Chip was a gunship pilot and Mr. Rice was to be a MedEvac pilot and would be flying medical evacuation missions, just as Roger and I would be doing. Chip would fly 'guns' and possibly fly UH1D troop lift helicopters. Once in-country, I would learn that gunships would simply be referred to as 'guns' and troop lift Hueys would be referred to as 'slicks'.

The four of us quickly became friends and wondered just what flying in Vietnam would be like. It became very apparent that Chip and George had a much better feel for what we were about to encounter than either Roger or myself. The fact was that both of them had spent a great deal of time training at Ft. Benning prior to our deployment. To put it mildly, Roger and I would be learning as we went along.

Our route to Vietnam would be south, crossing through the Panama Canal, west to Hawaii and on to Qui Nhon Harbor, South Vietnam. We were told that depending on the en route weather, the voyage would take 26-30 days. Later on, we were told that the time spent en route would count towards our one year tour in Vietnam. That was pleasant news, but due to a later snafu, Roger and I didn't really get the credit. More about that later.

After going through what I would describe as the 'eastern locks' of the Panama Canal and entering the large open lake area prior to reaching the Pacific Ocean, I returned to my quarters and went to sleep. When I awoke and went out on deck, we were well into the open seas of the Pacific. It was quite a strange feeling to me, but very calming with a star-filled sky. I guess the strange feeling was a result of knowing that I was getting further and further away from my family and my country.

Days later, just prior to reaching Pearl Harbor, an announcement came over the ship's loud speaker that we would be remaining overnight in Hawaii and would most likely be allowed to depart the ship. Having been on board for about 18 days, this was naturally music to our ears. The four of us began to make plans as to what we would do while off the ship in Honolulu. Without going into all the details, we decided to 1) get one large hotel room at Waikiki Beach, 2) set up a fully-stocked bar in the room, and 3) hit the beach.

We docked in Pearl Harbor at about 0900 hours. Shortly thereafter, we were officially notified that we would be allowed to depart the ship until 2400 hours that night. We were also informed that the ship would be departing the next morning at 0800 hours. We understood our curfew of 2400 hours but we also realized that the ship would not be leaving until eight hours later. At that point, the four of us decided that as long as we were back to the ship before 0800 the next morning, we should be OK.

Just before departing the ship around 1030 hours, another announcement came over the PA system that 'liberty' would expire at 0800 hours the next morning. We all knew that message was for any ship crew members that were being allowed off the ship, but it further solidified the fact that we definitely would not be returning that night at 2400 hours. I said to my three bunk mates, "Fellows, that seals the deal for me!" All agreed.

Once off the ship, we secured a cab and the four of us departed for Waikiki Beach. We booked our suite at the Hawaiian Village Hotel, immediately secured our 'adult beverages' at the Ft. Derussy Class VI store, set up our bar, and headed for the beach. It didn't take long for the four of us to start attracting attention and before we knew it, our table for four at the hotel beach bar had turned into two tables being pushed together accommodating five or six locals, male and female.

As the day/party progressed with drinking, eating, swimming, talking, etc., it was obvious that everyone was having fun and enjoying themselves in their own way. Every so often, one could hear plans being made by different individuals for the evening. Such planning further solidified in my mind that my three friends and I would not be returning to the ship that night at 2400 hours. I was told nothing different by any of my three buddies.

During the afternoon, I was invited to have dinner at one of the restaurants near the hotel. After dinner, around 2130 hours, I returned to the hotel room only to find our bar empty. I just figured that in my absence, the party at the outside bar had moved to another room or location. I checked the outside bar to see if any of the afternoon crowd, including my three buddies, were still there. They weren't. I decided to walk up to the International Market Place, a famous tourist attraction at the time, to see what was going on.

I returned to our suite around 0100 hours and again, found no one there. I called the front desk for a wake-up call and taxi for 0700 the next morning and went to sleep. The next morning I received my wake-up call, and again noticed that I was the only one that had spent the night in our room. Still being a bit 'buzzed' from the night before, I was in a happy mood. I showered, dressed, and checked out of the room, found my taxi, and departed for the ship.

Upon arriving in the big black limo taxi, I immediately noticed three things. One, the sizable stairway to exit and board the ship was gone. Two, there was no one else waiting to board the ship. And three, there were a large number of troops already on board the ship taking my picture as I walked away from the taxi. At this point, I did notice at the far end of the ship what looked like a small bridge/plank going into the lower deck of the ship. I walked toward that area, all the while having guys take my picture. It was quite dark inside the ship where I entered.

But as soon as I entered, someone grabbed me by the arm and said, "Lieutenant Covington, where the hell have you been?"

I saw that the person was a major and I said, "Waikiki Beach, sir."

He then said, "Your commander will be talking with you."

I said, "Yes, sir," and proceeded to look for my quarters. It dawned on me later that even though it was dark in the area where I entered the ship, the major still called me by name. I later found out that I had been the last troop to get back on the ship, and by three to four hours at that. So much for the picture taking.

As for the missing adult beverages in our hotel room, I later learned that one of my three bunk buddies had gotten a bit upset about something that happened after I departed our Waikiki Beach afternoon festivities. In retaliation, he scarfed up all the room beverages and returned to the ship well before 2400 hours. After hearing all the details of what supposedly happened and seeing how hung over our 'beverage culprit' was, all was forgiven. After all, we were on our way to Vietnam.

The remainder of the voyage was highlighted with the receipt of our Gama Globulin shots, one in each cheek of our backsides. It seemed forever before the swelling subsided and allowed one to be comfortable sitting down or sleeping on one's back. In fact, a few encounters broke out when a playful slap on the butt was delivered by one who was thought to be your friend. Other highlights included viewing the movie, "Viva Las Vegas" with Elvis and Ann Margaret six or seven times and occasionally seeing the only live female on board, a pussy cat that someone had smuggled on before leaving Hawaii. And no, there was no chastity belt attached to the cat.

On or about 28 days after leaving Savannah, Georgia, the announcement came over the PA system that we would be arriving in Qui Nhon Harbor, South Vietnam the next day. A cheer went up throughout the ship regardless of the fact that we all knew that we were about to enter a combat zone. It appeared that everyone was more than ready to get off the Upshur.

As I mentioned earlier, since it was late July 1965 with the big buildup in Vietnam just beginning, there were only a small number of Vietnam veterans on board. In fact, none of our fifty or so 498th Air Ambulance Company Officer and Enlisted personnel had previously served in Vietnam. Any Vietnam veterans on board were all members of the 1st Air Cav. I mention this fact because not long after the announcement about our arrival the following day, I felt a bit of apprehension and saw the same in a lot of other eyes. Things were definitely quieter and more serious on board. Yes, we were about to enter a war.

CHAPTER FOUR

AUGUST, 1965

1ST TOUR – SOUTH VIETNAM

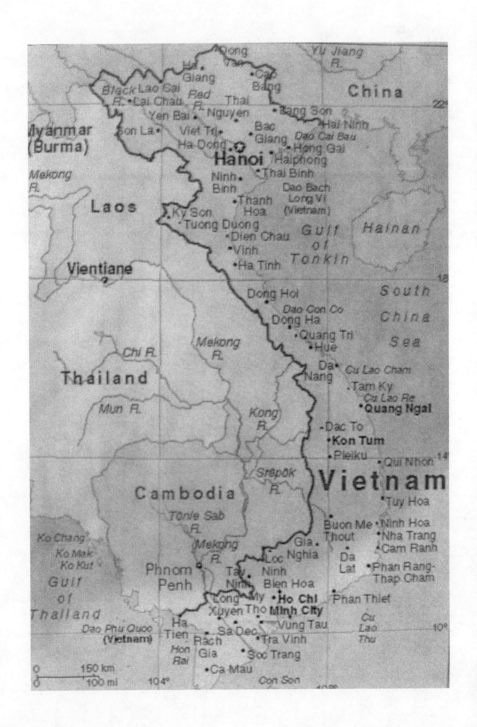

Awakening the next morning, I went out on deck to find that we were anchored and in the harbor. Since you may not be familiar with Qui Nhon, which is located in the II Corps area of South Vietnam, I will describe the area. The airfield is located right near the beach, with Qui Nhon adjacent to the north. There is a small mountain/ridge just to the south of the airfield. I immediately noticed two fixed wing aircraft dropping bombs on the upper part of the ridgeline. This close proximity of action really got my attention since two of our flight platoons with 12 of our UH1D helicopters would be located on the nearby airfield. I would find out later that the two aircraft dropping the ordinance were Vietnamese Air Force A1E Sky Raiders that were attempting to take out some enemy snipers dug into the ridgeline. The A1E's must have been successful since no more bombing took place in that area after our landing.

That morning, we were informed that we would be joining the 1st Air Cav personnel in departing the ship on small landing craft to go ashore, then to the airfield staging area. As the day progressed, and with the Navy landing craft transporting personnel to the beach, I could see a lot of Chinook (CH-47) helicopters landing and taking off from the airfield, having been told on board the ship by some of the 1st Cav personnel that once they got to the airfield, they would be airlifted inland to a place called An Khe. That fact accounted for all of the helicopter traffic at the Qui Nhon airfield.

Our 498th personnel had been told that our unit advance party, which had been flown earlier to Nha Trang, Vietnam, would send someone to meet us at the airfield. They were also supposed to have living quarters waiting for us. Our Headquarters, 1st Platoon and Maintenance Station, would be located at Nha Trang. Our 2nd and 3rd Platoons would be located at Qui Nhon and our 4th Platoon at Pleiku in the Central Highlands. Each Platoon was authorized six UH1D helicopters and the required officer and enlisted personnel.

Upon arrival at the airfield, our fifty or so 498th personnel were provided an area to assemble and wait for our representative from our Advance Party to contact us. A couple of our 498th Majors informed us to relax and stay put while they went to look for our contact. Not long after they left, a 1st Cav Major came up and said for us to get ready to board a Chinook to be transported to An Khe. Being fairly close to the Major, I informed him that we were not members of the 1st Cav, but were 498th Air Ambulance Company personnel to be stationed at Qui Nhon.

Before I could tell him that two of our Majors had left to look for our Advance Party contact, he said, "Lieutenant, you came on the ship with the 1st Cav, you're going to An Khe with the Cav." He departed the area in a bit of a grumpy mood.

As for the 1st Cav Division, I have always had tremendous respect for them. Notwithstanding, I had also heard while on the Upshur that An Khe was still in the process of being prepared in order to receive the 1st Cav troops. Additionally, I heard that the vast majority of troops would be living for quite a while in pup tents. This fact and the statement by the Major really got my attention.

A bit later, our Majors returned stating that they had not been able to find anyone from our Advance Party nor anyone that knew where we might be quartered in the area. We passed on what the 1st Cav Major had told us about going to An Khe and their response was, "No way."

I had previously seen a couple of box ambulances parked not too far away from our location. I asked permission from one of the Majors to go and see what medical units were in the area. He said, "Go ahead."

Upon speaking with one of the ambulance drivers, I learned that they were stationed at the airfield to transport patients and medical personnel to and from an evacuation hospital that was located in a valley about thirty minutes outside of Qui Nhon. I asked the driver if I could catch a ride on the next trip to the hospital. He said, "No problem."

Having no place for our personnel to stay, the Major said, "Go ahead and check out the hospital." Later on, upon arriving at the hospital, not only did I learn that it was my old unit, the 85th Evac from Ft. Chaffee, but that a lot of the personnel that I had previously served with were still in the unit. Greetings were exchanged and I relayed the situation that our unit personnel were in. I was told by one of the 85th Evac personnel that they would erect a couple of additional tents for us until we got our situation straightened out. They said they would also send transportation if the situation was the same for us when I returned to the airfield.

Once back at the airfield, I learned that the situation was the same – no place to stay. I said, "No worry, we can stay with the 85th Evac in the valley." I became an instant hero without flying one medical evacuation mission in country. Not only were we all well received by the 85th personnel, they planned a party for the following night. I would later learn that just about any out of the ordinary positive happening in the medical community could result in some form of a spontaneous party.

We stayed two nights in the valley with the 85th before being advised that our Advance Party contact had arrived and secured quarters on the airfield for both our enlisted and officer personnel. The quarters were Quonset type, half wood and half screen with tin roofs. They were very adequate and most definitely better than what the 1st Cav troops would be living in at An Khe. A few days later, the Navy carrier with our UH1D helicopters arrived, the aircraft were made ready for flight, and we went to the ship and flew them to our designated helipad area on one of the Qui Nhon airfield ramps.

As an in-country orientation, some of us flew a few medevac missions with a Transportation Corps unit that had been assigned to the area to support aeromedical missions prior to our arrival. All went well during that brief period of time. Now with our 12 UH1D helicopter MSC aviators, our enlisted personnel (which included our crew chiefs, medical corpsman, electronics, maintenance and supply), we were ready to perform our area support aeromedical evacuation mission. Our call sign would be 'Dustoff'.

By this time, some other events had occurred. The 85th Evac hospital had relocated from the valley outside of Qui Nhon to the airfield. South Vietnam units (ARVN) were steadily increasing in the area and were being supported by a Marine CH 34 Helicopter Squadron for our assault missions. Units of the 101st Airborne Division, some of which had preceded the 1st Cav into the An Khe area for clearing/securing purposes, were becoming much more active in search and destroy missions. Helicopter gunship teams, mostly B model UH1s, were arriving at the airfield. It should be noted that prior to mid-1965, the majority of combat action on the ground was taking place in the III and IV Corps areas of South

Vietnam. These two areas combined made up the southern half of South Vietnam with me and II Corps making up the northern half. With the 1st Air Cav and the 101st Airborne Division arriving in the II Corps area, the 'war zone' was now being extended northward.

With twelve UH1Ds assigned to our two platoons, sixteen pilots available/twenty-four authorized, it was necessary to secure some additional pilots. We were able to get some branch immaterial, i.e., Infantry, TC Corp, Engineers, etc. and some Warrant Officer pilots. They were all welcomed to our unit and were a Godsend.

With the American and ARVN Forces steadily increasing in the II Corps area, it quickly became apparent that the Vietcong and North Vietnamese (NVA) were also increasing and becoming much more active. The combat action and casualties on both sides were increasing at a very fast rate. In order to meet the requirements of our area support aeromedical mission, we had two crews on 24-hour duty at Que Nhon, plus a third up crew on basically daytime duty. The 1st and 2nd up 24-hour duty crews took the field pickup missions on a rotational basis and the day crew was responsible for hospital to hospital transfers. We also had two crews on field standbys – one at Tuy Hoa and one at Ban Me Thuot. If there was an American or ARVN search and destroy operation going on in the Bong Son area, we would have a crew on station there also. Bong Son was a 30 to 35 minute flight north, northwest of Qui Nhon. The field standbys were usually three to four days in length before you were relieved by another crew.

As stated before, we only started with sixteen pilots in our two combined platoons at Qui Nhon, and it took some time before we received the twenty-four pilots that we were authorized. With ten to twelve pilots required to fly per day, you can see that we were quite busy flying our medical evacuation missions.

We also had other administrative type officer requirements to perform and those were normally accomplished by the more senior majors and captains. So Jerry Spruiell, Roger Hula, the now-assigned warrant officers and I got to do a great deal of the flying. I personally liked that because I wanted and needed as much flying experience as I could get. The fact was that I only had around twenty-five hours of UH1D time when I arrived in Vietnam. Hula, Spruiell and I quickly became Aircraft Commanders (AC) and that was also fine with me.

Additional pilots were being periodically assigned to our two platoons, a few branch immaterial, but mostly young warrant officers. They were a great asset and really appreciated. We had now been in-country almost two months and even though we had had a number of aircraft hit by enemy fire, we had not had any crew members wounded. But we all knew that fact would not likely last forever.

Major Burroughs, Lt. Roger Hula, the crew chief and flight medic were making an ARVN pickup in what was supposed to be a secure area just west of Qui Nhon. As they were exiting the pickup site, they began receiving enemy fire and Major Burroughs was hit in the neck area, knocking him off of the controls. It was our Standard Operating Procedure (SOP) for one pilot to be flying the helicopter during field pickups and takeoffs, with the other pilot lightly on the controls in case something happened. During the short period of Lt. Hula taking full control of the aircraft, one of the helicopter skids struck a palm tree while exiting the area. This fact was evidenced by both blood and debris still on the skid upon landing at the 85th Evac in Qui Nhon. Major Burroughs was not fatally wounded, but was permanently evacuated from Vietnam. Even though he lost some ability to speak due to the damage to his larynx, he eventually regained his full speaking ability. Off the record, it was decided that the entire crew should get credit for a kill (enemy in palm tree) or at least the wounding of one of the enemy.

Not very long after this incident, we had three aircraft involved in making some field pickups of gunshot wounds in an area outside of Qui Nhon called 'Choppy Bobbin'. We had some gunship support as their fuel allowed, due to the amount of armament and ammunition they carried. My aircraft had already been shot up once departing one of the pickup sites and I had to get a replacement aircraft. We knew the area was 'hot' and I felt it necessary to use every technique that ILT Ernie Sylvester had taught me earlier at Ft. Sam Houston.

Returning to the area to pickup more casualties with my replacement aircraft, and getting ready for a descent to land in a pickup site marked by smoke, I received this radio transmission from one of the gunship team leaders, "Dustoff, get your ass on the deck so we can cover you and not get someone killed."

I recognized that the gunship team leader was Lt. Jim Vance, a man that I grew to respect more and more as he and his team members flew cover for me and my crewmembers. I only wish Colonel Madrano could have been on the scene to see first-hand not only what was expected, but needed to greatly decrease our chances of being hurt.

Our three crews were able to successfully get all the wounded out of the area and to the 85th Evac on a timely basic with no one dying or losing a limb.

My aircraft did take some more hits but no one was injured. In this particular case, the Vietcong (VC) was in a 'spider trap' very near the pickup site. He had been undiscovered by the ground troops and waited until we were loading patients to raise up and open fire. I learned later on that he was killed and can only figure that he must have gotten a bit irritated hearing or seeing our wounded being evacuated. All the hits we received were in the tail section of the aircraft so I guess the VC was attempting to take out our tail rotor blade. Glad he missed.

While in operations monitoring the radios and waiting for the other aircraft to return, another one of our pilots involved in some of the pickups, but at different locations in the Choppy Bobbin area, came into Operations. Not knowing that my crew and I had taken hits a second time in the area, he commented, "It's a piece of cake out there, nothing's going on."

Shortly thereafter, his crew chief came into Ops holding the left pilot's cockpit door and pointing at a sizable hole in the top part of it. Due to the fact that this pilot was quite a tall person, the round had to pass just above his head. Seeing this, his idea of the security of the area quickly changed. As a matter of fact, it wasn't too very long before he began to have vision problems resulting in him being restricted to hospital to hospital flying only, with no field pickups.

That initially bothered both me and some others because as inexperienced as we were in combat flying, we expected to be shot at in a war zone. As I gained more experience and saw certain other things happen, I became a bit more understanding of such situations. As my younger brother, Ralph, a guidance counselor, has always said to me, "Bill, everyone is different and may react differently to any given situation."

Later that afternoon, the requests for urgent medevacs continued to come in. I want to relate a serious incident that happened to my flight medic during one of our pickups. Even though we preferred the ground unit personnel to have their wounded located close together in order to reduce ground time, that was not always possible due to enemy fire in the area. In order to stay in radio contact with both our flight medic and crew chief while on the ground, we had extended radio cords. But on this particular pickup, our flight medic was going to have to unhook his cord in order to get to some of the patients. He asked for permission to unhook and I said, "OK."

One can see how important it is for all crew members to be in communication while on the ground, since you may have to quickly leave the area unexpectedly. You want to make sure all of your crew members are on board the aircraft because you never want to leave anyone on the ground. Another point was, with lots of noise, i.e., rotor blades, engine radio chatter, friendly and/or enemy fire, etc., it's not always obvious that you may be taking fire. After a short period of time, feeling that the medic should have secured the remaining patient, I called for a response. No answer was received. Over my right shoulder, I could see that the CE was busy positioning the patients on board the aircraft. Still not receiving a response from my flight medic, I leaned further over in my seat so I could see where I figured our flight medic should be by this time. This is what I saw. My medic was standing beside the open, sliding door, eyes very wide open, looking and yelling at me, periodically pointing at the door, and simultaneously attempting to connect his radio cord. I didn't notice any more patients to be loaded and hearing the ground radio operator saying, "Dustoff, get out of the area", I motioned for the flight medic to board the aircraft. He did.

Lifting out of the pickup site and staying treetop level, the flight medic came on the intercom and in a very excited voice said, "Sir, a bullet just missed my head back there on the ground." Both my co-pilot and I immediately looked again at all the aircraft instruments. They were all reading properly, and we breathed a sigh of relief. I informed the crew chief that the aircraft seemed to be OK. I confirmed with the medic that we had gotten all of the patients as he was already in the process of administering aid.

At this point, let me elaborate on just how skilled our flight medics actually were. It goes without question that they and the ground medics played a key role in the saving of individual lives and limbs during the Vietnam War. If the situation or time permitted, the ground medic played the initial role in the medical evacuation sequence. But oftentimes, the fact was at the time of our Dustoff arrival, the ground medic had not had the time to render aid to all the wounded. In such cases, our flight medic, while en route to the hospital, would perform these initial life and limb saving procedures. This was not done in a stable environment, but in a turning, vibrating helicopter. Keeping that in mind, these ground and flight medics can never get enough credit for their services in Vietnam.

Once we reached the 85th Evac, we shut the aircraft down and sure enough, one of the hits had struck the sliding door, just inches away from where the flight medic was standing. None of the hits we received caused any major damage to the aircraft and with some '100 mile an hour'/strong tape, we were ready to fly again. By this time, our medic had calmed down, but it had been quite obvious that the bullet near his head had totally gained his attention at what could be described as a 'moment of truth'.

Fortunately, all went well the remainder of the day and we had some laughs, including our medic, at my description of his frantic attempt to reconnect his radio cord during all the excitement on the ground during the pickup.

Qui Nhon airfield was not a bad place to be based. Our living quarters were adequate with enough fans to keep us comfortable both day and night. The fans also kept the mosquitoes from being able to land and take a bite. Mosquito nets were available but not normally used. In fact, I don't remember anyone, officer or enlisted, contracting malaria during my tour. We would periodically take the malaria pills, which always induced extra latrine visits, at least by me.

Being a part of the medical team, the 85th Evac would occasionally have a party and invite us. They, having the female nurses, helped us not lose sight of just how much we loved and appreciated our wives and/or girlfriends back home. Now, that is a positive statement with reference to both the nurses, our wives, and/or our girlfriends back home. You figure out what I mean.

Our dining facility/mess hall was just across the street from our officer hooches, but we were also allowed to go into Qui Nhon Village to eat if we liked. But it was frowned upon. Even though our field grade/majors were billeted in a villa outside of the airfield perimeter, one of the officers, Major Nash, elected to stay on the airfield.

By this time, I had formed a fairly close friendship with Major Nash. Since he enjoyed eating in the village, I would frequently join him for some of our meals. He played a number of musical instruments, one of which was the saxophone. Word got around and he was invited to play in some of the local Vietnamese bands. On some occasions, he would invite me to go with him when I was not on a field standby or local flight duty. We would eat in some of the local village cafes and I never got sick.

I say that boastfully, because I can still see the kitchen personnel rinsing off previously used plates, bowls and utensils with cold water from a rubber hose and then immediately using said items for other customers. The food was obviously fresh and well-cooked in order to prevent any germs and/or diseases from being spread. I guess my strong stomach also helped quite a bit.

One other significant note about our food consumption in Vietnam. Two of my favorite army issue items were the dehydrated shrimp that came in one gallon cans. One can, when boiled, produced lots and lots of very tasty shrimp, as long as you had some sauce such as cocktail or ketchup. The other excellent item was frozen steaks by the case. For certain favors, we were able to get both of these tasty items on a fairly regular basis. The fact of the matter was that I know that I ate more steak and shrimp on my two tours in Vietnam than I had in my entire life up until that time. Our field troops obviously did not fare so well, often only having C-rations on their missions, but I know there was a big effort to get them hot meals as often as possible. Overall, everyone ate fairly well.

The CH34 Marine Squadron had a small Officer's Club at the end of our street on the airfield. They invited us to come and enjoy when we had time off. Being the only Officer's Club available at the time, we didn't hesitate. The two things that I remember the most vividly about the club were a young Vietnamese bartender nicknamed 'Miss Snow'. She was quite pretty and spoke relatively good English. Supposedly, she was 'off limits' to all patrons of the club. That said, she was constantly being hit on by some customers. An interesting thing about her was that she was always very courteous, humble, and graceful in turning her admirers down in whatever proposition they might offer.

Another thing that I noticed about Miss Snow was that she had some scars just above her ankles. I later learned that she and her family had to leave their farm outside of Qui Nhon due to the Viet Cong and the war activity. The scars were from leeches she encountered while harvesting rice from the paddies on the family farm. Since leaving Vietnam, I have often wondered what happened to Miss Snow after the war. I sure hope that she survived and is OK.

The other thing that I vividly remember about the club was that on one occasion when I dropped in to have a beer or two, one of our majors was wearing a marine beret. When I asked him why, he simply said, "It was a gift." I later learned that he and a marine had had a disagreement over something resulting in the exchange of a few blows. Not remembering what they had argued about, they simply exchanged hats as a gesture of future friendship. To this day, that has sort of signified the camaraderie that I continuously observed during my two years in Vietnam.

Our two platoons at Qui Neon were fully manned crew-wise and we were staying extremely busy after a couple of months in-country. The big buildup was continuing at a rapid pace. We were flying lots of missions and evacuating lots of patients. All was going well, but that was about to change.

I was off-duty one night when the word came in that we had one of our Dustoff crews down. Despite my rush to get to our operations building, my thoughts and hopes were that no one had been hurt. Our second up was preparing to launch. The weather was marginal, but flyable. That night we had three of our enlisted crew members—a flight medic, a crew chief, and a gunner – all killed in the accident. Both of our pilots received burns and one also received a broken ankle. This was late 1965 and our UH1Ds did not have crashworthy fuel cells. Our two pilots were evacuated to the 85th Evac and later on to Japan.

As I stated before, the weather was marginal and the information that was received later was that just before touchdown, the aircraft entered a fog bank, hit the ground, crashed and burned. Our two pilots, one a major and one a captain, were both very experienced helicopter pilots. They were never second-guessed about their attempt to complete their medical evacuation mission. The majority of us had already flown in marginal weather conditions and knew that such conditions would happen again, more likely sooner than later.

Right or wrong, it's a fact that when you know some wounded soldier's life is depending on you and your crews going that extra step beyond the normal, you do it. Hopefully, that attitude will never change with our Dustoff medevac crews. It's dangerous, but not getting someone to a hospital that could die or lose a limb, is even worse. And you know what? I fully believe that our three crewmembers who lost their lives would agree with me if they were still alive. God rest their souls.

FIELD STANDBYS

TUY HOA

You could always expect action while on a field standby at Tuy Hoa. At any given time, you would have ARVN, White Horse Division (Koreans), and the 101st Airborne Division in the area conducting 'search and destroy' missions. At the time, none of these forces had their own aeromedical evacuation support in the area, so we supported them with our 'on station' field standby aircraft. Depending on the action, we would have one or two Dustoff aircraft on station.

I had a number of memorable days flying at Tuy Hoa but one of the most exciting went something like this.

My crew and I were evacuating wounded for both the ARVN and the 101st Airborne. Both units were in heavy contact. My aircraft had been shot up, requiring a replacement from Qui Nhon. Upon receipt of the new aircraft, we continued to fly missions. I have noted that the gunships had to refuel and re-arm on a more frequent basic than our Dustoff aircraft. We were en route to a pickup site on another mission. The gunships were returning to Tuy Hoa to refuel and re-arm and our patients were of the urgent category. Knowing that I was not going to wait for the guns to return to the medevac site, I made a radio call over the 'guard frequency' to see if there were any more gunship support in the area that could give us cover on this pickup. A FAC (Forward Air Control) aircraft pilot answered asking me the coordinates of the wounded and my ETA (estimated time of arrival) at the coordinates. I gave him the information and said I would be standing by.

Gunship coverage on hot missions is so important to Dustoff crews in so many ways. First, you have air observation in case you get shot up or shot down and someone can pinpoint your location in case you, your crew, and your on-board patients needed evacuating. Second, a gunship crew can put down suppressive fire if you need it while performing your mission. And third, gunship presence in the area normally discourages the enemy from exposing their position by firing at you and your crew. All of these reasons were equally important.

Prior to our reaching the pickup site, the FAC radioed that he had us some gunship support. I figured he had contacted another Huey helicopter gunship team that wasn't busy at the time that could give us some cover. The FAC pilot asked if I would get smoke to mark the LZ and asked me to confirm our entry direction. He also asked approximately how far out from the pickup site we would be going low level on the deck. I gave all the information that he had requested and he said that he and the 'guns' would be monitoring our radio commo with the ground forces and watching for the smoke.

Nearing the pickup area, I contacted the ground radio operation, told them I had gunship coverage and asked them to pop smoke. I reaffirmed that the area was still insecure and confirmed the color of smoke. I then informed the radio operator to have the patients ready and that we would be on the ground in a couple of minutes.

We then descended to treetop level. At 100 knots and approximately 200 meters from the pickup site, I felt our aircraft shake a bit and at the same time, observed two F4C Phantom jets, one on each side of and just above our level, flaps down, go whizzing by. At the time, I was flying the aircraft with my co-pilot monitoring the controls. Being a bit surprised at our gunship support, I almost overshot the pickup site. A forward, followed by a side flare, with a hammerhead pedal turn saved the day.

While sitting on the ground, the FAC pilot came over the radio and asked how we liked the gun coverage going into the area and would we like the same coming out of the LZ. I fully collected myself and said, "Thanks, but no thanks." He laughed and said he and his 'gun team' would stick around until we safely cleared the area. I thanked him and in my mind, I know that he and his four F4C jet pilots still laugh about the time they escorted a Dustoff crew on a medevac mission. All in all, we really did appreciate the support and I often wonder just what our ground troops and especially the enemy located in the immediate area thought about such close air support on such a mission.

BAN ME THUOT

Ban Me Thuot was basically a relatively easy standby mission except for one troubling factor. Flying south anytime (especially at night) over triple canopy jungle in a single-engine helicopter could and should get anyone's attention. On such missions, it was amazing how the engine and transmission instruments always seemed to flutter a bit more than normal. Thankfully, the good ol' UH1D Bell Helicopter never once failed for any of our 498th personnel while in the Ban Me Thuot area. Other than the night flying south out of Ban Me Thuot, one other event happened to me that was a bit exciting.

At our arrival briefing, my crew and I were informed that there had been some enemy perimeter probing and that a mortar attack on the compound was expected sometime soon. Two nights later, while watching the evening movie at the dining facility with a full house, someone decided to see what the reaction would be if he/they threw some fairly large rocks on the tin roof of the facility. The expected reaction worked in the fact that in record time, we moviegoers emptied the building in search of the nearest bunker. Our crew departed for Qui Nhon three days later with no mortar attack occurring, and the ransom on the culprit/culprits not being collected by anyone. As I stated before, Ban Me Thuot was normally a sedate area, and I guess someone was looking for a little excitement.

BONG SON

We would only have a field standby at Bon Song if some major American or Vietnamese offensive was planned. Not long after arriving in Qui Nhon, we were alerted that a mass casualty situation had occurred in the Bong Son area. We would learn later that the ARVN units in the area had been on a 'search and destroy' mission, but that their initial intelligence reports were that very little enemy contact was expected. Not knowing how many casualties to expect, we launched two Dustoff aircraft from Qui Nhon.

On that day, with additional aircraft, we evacuated well over 100 casualties, with the majority being KIA's (killed in action). I still remember the scene quite vividly. The KIA's had been brought out of the jungle and lined up along a very straight road which led into the Bon Song Pass. We formed a traffic pattern with one aircraft at a time landing on the road to pick up the KIA's. We basically just worked our way down the road until all were evacuated. Being so new in-country, I didn't think much about what was happening at the time. The fact was that this would be the largest amount of casualties, KIA's or survivors, that I would experience in a given day while in Vietnam. And it happened very early in my 1st tour.

Later on, I was on a field standby in Bong Son. My crew and I were alerted to accompany a command and control helicopter on a mission to the Bon Song Pass. The word from a unit commander was that radio contact had been lost with one of his outposts located in the Pass. He stated that his C&C ship would be landing in the Pass without radio contact and did not know what to expect. He wanted to see what was going on with his personnel. We would be observing the landing and would remain at altitude. No gunships were available in the area at the time and the commander felt it was urgent to see about his men.

Upon arrival at the pass, the C&C ship radioed that they would do a low level flyby to see if they could spot anyone first, then they intended to land. No one was observed on the low level flyby and the C&C ship stated that they would now land to determine just what was going on in the area. On the landing attempt, I observed that just before coming to a hover prior to landing, the C&C pilot radioed that they were taking fire.

En route back to Bong Son, we learned that the aircraft had taken hits and that the commander on board the aircraft had been wounded. Fortunately, no one was killed and I later found out that the outpost troops, for safety purposes, had gone 'radio silent', and were in the process of moving to a more secure area. This word had not been heard back at Bong Son and the fact that some enemy troops had occupied the abandoned Pass area was also unknown.

1st AIR CALVARY

Since we were basically an area support Aeromedical Evacuation Unit, the majority of our missions for the Cav was transporting their personnel from the 2nd surgical hospital at An Khe to the 85th Evac hospital at Qui Nhon. These missions were referred to as 'milk runs' since there was little or no danger involved. Our 3rd up Dustoff aircraft at Qui Nhon would normally handle these missions.

At this point, I want to relate a few significant differences between the 1st Air Cav 'Medevac' and our 498th Air Ambulance 'Dustoff'.

Their 15th Aeromedical Company consisted of 12 UH1Ds, solely in support of the 1st Air Cav Troops. Our 498th Aeromedical Company consisted of 25 UH1Ds in an area support mission of a number of different units, both American and Foreign Services. On occasion, we in the 498th would be placed in direct support of a particular unit, but this was the exception and not the rule. Their UH1Ds had two mounted M-60 machine guns, and we would sometimes add a gunner to our crew with a hand-held M-60. As stated above, their call sign was 'Medevac' and ours was 'Dustoff'.

I would have been proud to have served in the 1st Air Cav as a Medical Service Corps Pilot, but in retrospect, it was probably best for me that I didn't. The fact that on both of my tours in Vietnam, my living conditions were very adequate and those of my Medevac comrades were not, was not the reason for my feelings. There are a number of decisions to be made and often times different ways to successfully complete a field aeromedical evacuation mission, especially when the pickup site is insecure.

I will list a few of these considerations: 1) enemy activity and location, if known; 2) condition of and number of patients; 3) gunship support; 4) WX conditions; and 5) consolidation of patients in pickup site. All are important considerations on all combat field evacuations, but especially when enemy fire is expected.

Before I go any further, I want to clarify one thing about me and my Dustoff crews. That being, if it were reported by the ground unit that a patient or patient's wounds were life-threatening, regardless of the enemy situation, my decision as the Aircraft Commander (AC) was that we would immediately make a 100% effort to get the patient(s) out of harm's way. In my mind, the only factors that would stop me and my crewmembers would be extremely hazardous weather conditions or getting so shot up on the approach to the area that continuing would only further jeopardize my crew and the intended patients. This comment of getting severely shot up on approach into the pickup site happened only once to me during my two tours.

The point I want to make is that the environment that I flew in as a member of the 498th never caused me and my crews to be second-guessed by any other helicopter pilots. Those 'medevac' pilots in the 1st Air Cav would normally have a number of other helicopter pilots in the immediate area, some just waiting for the chance to show how brave they were. It is not up to me nor do I desire to criticize any of those involved in such a situation. I will just say that I am very thankful that I wasn't a part of any such actions.

Now back to one of the days that one of my Majors and I were on a field standby and in direct support of the 1st Air Cav on one of their 'search and destroy' missions. The AO (Area of Operation) was east/northeast of the An Khe Pass and was known as 'Happy Valley'. Why that name, I have no clue, except for the fact that any of the units that fought in this area were actually happy when the operation ended and they were able to vacate the place.

The Major, myself and our crew knew that we were in for some heavy action when the word came back to the medical clearing company that a number of troop assault helicopters had been shot up with a few going down in the LZ.

As the day progressed and during one of our Dustoff missions, I heard one of the 1st Cav pilots, who had just been shot down in the LZ, radio, "Hell, don't worry about getting us out of here. With all of us additional flight crew members now on the ground, I think we have the bastards outnumbered."

Of all the statements of and/or about the 1st Air Cav that I have ever heard, I think that one has impressed me the most. What a great fighting force!

Just to emphasize how much more difficult I think it was for the 1st Air Cav medevac unit and other such field units as compared to our Dustoff units, I will relate a couple of other stories to maybe enlighten you.

Even though our field units, such as the 1st Cav, did have high priority on certain items, it quickly became obvious that some were lacking. I will never forget seeing one of my fellow MSC aviators, Guy Kimsey, a member of the 1st Cav's aeromedical platoon, as he was in our unit area in Qui Nhon one day. Even though it was quite early in both our tours, his combat boots were almost completely worn out.

I asked him, 'Why such bad boots?"

He simply replied, "Boots are in short supply right now in the Cav."

I don't remember how many pairs of boots our unit scrounged up for Guy to take back to his unit, but I know they were all greatly appreciated.

Something that I never brought up with any of my friends that were assigned to the 1st Cav, but it was not uncommon to be told by your crew chief that your assigned UH1D for the day was missing some component such as a rotor blade or battery and the required replacement was being installed. Such occurrences were definitely frowned upon but some understanding and tolerance was felt. It was usually suspected that someone from the 1st Cav had paid us a visit during the night before.

Not long after the deaths of our three enlisted crew members, I learned that Warrant Officer George Rice, a pilot flying medevac with the 15th Aeromed Company, 1st Cav, had been killed during a mission. Since we had spent twenty-nine days as bunkmates on the ship coming over to Vietnam, I had gotten to know him quite well. He was a very pleasant and caring individual. I was very saddened by the news of his death, but because of our three crewmembers and his dedication, I knew their passing gave me even more strength and desire to perform our 'mission of mercy' to the very best of my ability.

CHOPPY BOBBIN

The area we referred to as 'Choppy Bobbin' was no more than 20-25 minutes flight time from Qui Nhon. But on any given day, it could be a very exciting area to work and fly in. The excitement and concern while flying a mission under enemy fire really spiked one's adrenaline flow.

On this particular day, the U.S. ground forces were running low on ammunition. They also reported that their re-supply helicopter had taken hits and had not been heard from in some time. We received this ammo situation report just as we were descending out of altitude to get low level for our approach into the pickup site. I made an assumption, which almost always was bad, that our crew chief, flight medic and gunner (hand-held M-60 machine gun) had all monitored the low ammo situation on the ground. I informed the ground radio operator that we would help as much as we could on the ammo situation and to have the patients ready for pickup.

Our unit had a number of operating procedures for both pilots and crewmembers, but two stand out in my mind reference this situation. One, that all crewmembers monitor all transmissions so as to know what is going on and also not to interrupt important transmissions. Two, that we as aeromedical evacuation crews and in accordance with the Geneva Convention, do not operate as combat resupply aircraft. Regardless, I had no problem with giving the ground troops the extra M-60 ammo that we had on board. I knew we could get more back in Qui Nhon.

Just before touching down in the pickup site, I directed our gunner to "throw out all of your extra M-60 ammo."

The situation went something like this. All of the ground troops except for those assisting in loading the patients, were in the prone position and facing a tree line to the right rear of the helicopter. Some were firing toward the tree line. Just after we touched down, our gunner who was now on the ground began to fire his M-60 right over the heads of some of the ground troops. By the time I got him to stop firing, all of the ground troops to his front were really hugging the ground and some had their hands over their helmets. Our gunner finally understood that he needed to get his extra M-60 ammo out of the aircraft and to the combat troops. Fortunately, no one was injured with the additional covering fire rendered by our gunner.

Upon our departure, the ground radio operator said, "Thanks Dustoff, but next time, please don't attempt to increase our patient count."

Back at Qui Nhon, and after dropping off our patients at the 85th Evac, our gunner stated that when I said, "Throw out your M-60 ammo", he thought I meant for him to provide more covering fire. Needless to say, he had not monitored the requirement for ammo and I had not insured that he knew exactly what was expected once we landed in the area. Fact is, assumptions should not be made, especially when in tight situations.

Gaining experience almost on a daily basis, I felt that my flying was going well. I was an AC (Aircraft Commander) and had gained the confidence of my fellow pilots and crew members. I didn't feel that I was cocky, just confident about what I was doing. Well, believe you me, things can change in a heartbeat.

Remember, I came to Vietnam as a dual rated (fixed and rotary wing) fixed wing instrument rated aviator. Our two platoons were now receiving some young inexperienced helicopter pilots, most of which were right out of the Rotary Wing Warrant Officer Course at Ft. Rucker. They were new to combat flying, just as I had been a few months earlier.

Here is what happened. I had flown as AC with this young WO1 on a number of missions, both night and day. He appeared to have confidence in me and I felt the same way about him. On this particular night mission, the weather was such that a couple of artillery outposts assisted us by popping some parachute flares for visibility to help us in getting to our Korean pickup site. The weather was not perfect, but it was not bad and very flyable.

My method on approach into the pickup site, both night and day, was that either I or the co-pilot would fly the approach into the pickup site with the other flying the aircraft out of the area. Again, the pilot not actually flying the aircraft would be lightly on the controls and simultaneously monitoring the engine and flight instruments. Even though the pickup was to be made in a minimally lighted LZ, and in a mountainous area, it did not seem to pose any problem.

What happened to me on the letdown from altitude was that I concentrated so much on the flare pot lights marking the LZ that on final approach, I did not adequately monitor my altimeter or airspeed indicator. Consequently, on final approach, and quite a ways from my intended touchdown point, I had a nose-high aircraft attitude/angle and was actually very close to the ground. Continuing to descend, we hit the ground, again well short of the pickup site. The right skid caught some perimeter concertina wire and when I applied power, the aircraft rolled and we crashed.

At the time, there were five of us crewmembers on board the aircraft. My immediate thought was that I would be glad when the aircraft stops thrashing around so we could all exit. A post-crash fire was on my mind due to the fact that we still did not have crashworthy fuel cells.

Once outside the aircraft, I gathered the other four crewmembers and said, "We all need to get away from the aircraft in case of an explosion and/or fire."

It was dark and I immediately got tangled up in the concertina wire. Once I got untangled, we all got well away from the aircraft, which had not caught on fire. Everyone reported that they were OK except for cuts and bruises. When I asked who had their weapons, I learned that I was the only one, and that weapon was a .45 caliber pistol which I always had strapped on my chest. The other weapons had been displaced due to the crash. I believed that we were outside the Korean unit's perimeter due to the wire, but I wasn't sure.

In a short period of time, I heard some oriental voices. When I heard "Annyonghaseyo", I felt relieved because I recognized that to be Korean. My former 1st Sergeant at Ft. Chaffee, Arkansas had spent much of his military career in Korea and was always speaking the language. It was certainly a welcome feeling at the time to hear the language once again. Later that night, the patients and my crew and I were evacuated from the area back to Qui Nhon.

As you may be thinking, this was a very humbling experience for me. And it was, but I very quickly set forth to determine just what had happened to allow the accident to happen. As an AC, I made a number of mistakes. I will discuss the obvious ones. I had not been specific enough in telling my co-pilot exactly what I expected of him while I was flying the approach into the pickup site. A simple, "Keep me informed of the altitude and airspeed" could and probably would have kept us from hitting the ground. Also, I was concentrating so much on the LZ lights during the approach that I did not monitor either the altitude or the airspeed indicators. With the aircraft in a very nose-high angle on final, I had obviously felt that we were still a bit high so I continued to descend until striking the ground and concertina wire.

The next day, while discussing the accident with my co-pilot, he stated that having flown with me a number of times before, and even observing that I was extremely low on final approach, he felt that I knew what I was doing. Did I blame my co-pilot for what happened in any way? Not at all. It was totally my fault.

The following day, I was interviewed by a Flight Sergeant, took a post-accident checkride, and was back on the duty roster as an AC. I was very thankful that no one had been seriously hurt and have related the accident frequently to others. Hopefully, it helped them in preventing such an accident in the future.

Returning to any type of dangerous work after one experiences a mishap or an extremely close call, is an interesting topic. My attitude has always been that the longer one stays away from the hazardous environment, the tougher it is to effectively get back with the program. Well, it didn't take very long for me to get back into the thick of things. It was a day mission, and it proved to be plenty exciting.

I was flying with one of our Majors, Gib Beltran, who was an outstanding helicopter pilot. A convoy had been ambushed north of Qui Nhon on Route #1. The ambush took place just south of a small village called Phu My. En route, and with expected gunship support, we were informed by the convoy ground personnel that they were in the process of consolidating the wounded and they would contact us as soon as the patients were ready for pickup. They also gave the gunships and our Dustoff crew the location where the enemy fire had last come from.

Upon reaching the area, we established an orbiting pattern at 1,500 feet just west of the convoy location. The gunship flight leader stated that they were going to make a couple of firing runs on the tree line where the enemy fire had been reported. I was in the right pilot's seat watching the gunships make their runs. Suddenly, I saw one of the gunships pitch up and heard the transmission, "We are taking fire and going down."

I immediately informed Major Beltran, who transmitted to the gunship team leader that we would follow the shot up gunship down and pick up the crew. It should be noted that due to the expected number of wounded from the ambushed convoy, we had already requested a backup Dustoff from Qui Nhon. That aircraft was en route to the convoy location.

On short final into the downed aircraft location, we observed the extensive amount of water in the rice paddy where the damaged aircraft had landed. This fact dictated that we land approximately 30 yards away. By this time, the two gunners on the downed gunship had disengaged their M-60 machine guns and were putting fire into the tree line where the enemy was located.

Up until now, I had never had the opportunity to use my M-16 while on a mission. Since there was a problem with our flight medic quickly getting to the downed gunship, I figured this was a good time to assist with the suppressive fire. Again, observing where the gunship gunners were firing, I secured my M-16, stuck the barrel out my window and began firing in the direction of the tree line. I had raised my flight helmet visor in an effort to get better visibility. Upon firing my M-16, almost immediately one of the ejected cartridge cases hit me in my forehead. I was startled and thought I had been hit, so that quickly ended my suppressive fire. Naturally, I was quite relieved once I figured out what had happened.

Since it was taking quite a bit of time for our medic to start back to our Dustoff aircraft, I figured that some crew member had been either wounded by enemy fire or possibly injured during the landing. After a very lengthy amount of time, and being informed by our flight medic that one of the gunship pilots had been fatally wounded, we had everyone on board and departed for the hospital.

The gunship pilot had been fatally hit with a bullet that had passed through a small gap in the seat armor and had struck the pilot in the heart. Other Dustoff aircraft from our unit completed the initial medevac request involving the ambushed convoy.

PRAISE, BUT WITH A PRICE

Just because you and your crew successfully complete a difficult mission, help save some lives, and maybe even receive some gratitude and plaudits from the ground troops and your gunship escort, doesn't necessarily mean that you won't get an ass-chewing from your Commander.

As I have previously stated, I admired and respected Colonel Madrano both during and after my service in Vietnam. I still do today but he did have a way of putting things in perspective, which could very well question one's judgment abilities.

My crew and I received a request to evacuate an undetermined number of ARVN wounded from a hot LZ. Gunship escort was requested and approved. The gunship team leader was Lt. Jim Vance of the Dragons, one of my favorite gunship pilots. Upon arrival at the pickup site, we received the tactical situation, number and type of wounded, and I requested the ground unit to pop smoke for identification. The color of smoke was confirmed. The pickup site was a confined area on a short, narrow dirt road with lots of trees along each side. Now, if there is one thing that you want to do in reference to a hot LZ, it's to limit the number of trips you have to make into the area. Upon landing, our medic and crew chief began loading patients. The gunships were in a low level, figure-eight pattern providing cover.

Looking back in the cabin area, I confirmed that we were definitely with a full load of patients. Due to the expected weight, I figured that I would not be able to do anything close to a vertical takeoff and more than likely, the takeoff would be more of the low level, running type. Looking down the short road, I envisioned a running takeoff to get enough transitional lift to clear all the obstacles.

Getting a "Ready for takeoff" from the flight medic, I brought the aircraft to a low hover. We were heavy and reading just below maximum hovering power. I informed the gunships that we were exiting the area and began to move forward. As we began hovering down the short dirt strip, we got transitional lift but not enough to clear some of the smaller trees. As the rotor blades began to chop away some of the tree limbs and as we cleared the area, Lt. Vance came over the radio and transmitted, "Give 'em hell, Dustoff."

He had obviously observed the lawnmower action that had occurred during our takeoff. My exhilaration was short-lived in the fact that the next day, Colonel Madrano was visiting our two platoons in Qui Nhon and gave the word that he wanted to talk with me. The very one-sided conversation went something like this.

He said, "Bill, there once was a zoo that had a bear that everyone liked. But every now and then, the bear would get out of hand, tear up his cage, harass some of the patrons, and just cause too much trouble. Finally, the zoo management had to get rid of the bear. You don't want to be that kind of bear, do you?" Before I could answer, he went on to explain how much rotor blades cost and how hard they were to get on a timely basis. Thankfully, he never mentioned the helicopter that I had totally destroyed. I appreciated that and never once considered trying to defend my thinking about the one-time landing approach to Dustoff missions. To this day, I think that Lt. Vance, before my counseling session with Colonel Madrano, spoke up on my behalf to him. If so, I really appreciate that fact.

PERSONALITIES DIFFER

I have noted earlier that the 498th Air Ambulance Company arrived in South Vietnam with 25 new UH1D helicopters and 25 MSC aviators. Fairly early in the tour, we began to receive additional aviators, both commissioned and warrant officers. Many of these individuals stand out in my mind and I have already mentioned some of them in my stories. I now want to write about two more of my fellow combat aviators.

I want to relate these stories for a specific reason. That being, first impressions can be very deceiving, especially in combat. Both Ike Gray and Ed Monte caught my attention early on in their tours. Remember, my belief and attitude was that my crews and I were always going to survive, no matter how difficult the situation. As an AC, both Ed and Ike were assigned to fly with me on a number of missions.

Two things caught my eye. Ike appeared to be a bit more nervous than I thought to be normal and Ed always seemed to perspire more than usual, regardless of the difficulty of the mission. I never mentioned either of these observations to either Ed or Ike for two reasons. One, they both always performed admirably on missions and two, I never wanted either of them to feel that I was suspect in any way.

Since they were both going to have eight to nine months left on their one-year tours, I did ask a friend of mine how they both fared after I left country. He stated that they both did very well. I also found out later that the nervous appearance was simply Ike's nature and the same applied to Ed's perspiring. The situation really taught me to be very suspect of first impressions. They certainly can be deceiving.

PARTY TIME

I have already mentioned the fact that even in a war zone, there can be some humor and such happenings really do relieve a lot of the tension and anxiety one may encounter. On a number of occasions, we would get invited to some other unit's party. We decided to reciprocate and planned a party at our location which would include food, drinks and some type of music.

The plan called for all invitees to provide their own transportation to the party and we would provide the transportation back to their units. It was also understood that the party would be officers only and due to the limited space, only a few of our marine comrades would be invited. It should be noted that an explanation and agreement was made with our enlisted personnel, who were quartered just across the street from the party area. The agreement being that we would sponsor a party for them in the near future. All was well and understood.

We did have a safety concern about the fact that a number of female nurses from the 85th Evac hospital would be attending, and there would be a large number of male personnel in the area that would not be attending. Also, there was only one latrine facility in the immediate area so all the females that needed to use the facility were asked to take a male escort.

The party was going well until around 2100 hours when a blonde female nurse bounded in the back door of the party, hands on her head and bleeding profusely from the scalp area. This was not funny but with many of the attendees being from the medical community, she was quickly consoled, a head bandage applied, and she was immediately taken to the hospital for stitching. It was later confirmed that she elected to go to the latrine unescorted and was approached on her way back to the party. She undoubtedly said "no" to the culprit and no one was ever accused of the assault. And, oh yes, the music never stopped during the entire episode.

Now, let me tell you what I and many others considered the most humorous event of the evening. Around midnight, some of the attendees that were on duty the next morning needed transportation across the airfield to the hospital. I was standing outside the party facility observing some of the hospital personnel load into one of our jeeps. I heard one of our pilots state that he would ride shotgun on that particular trip.

Shortly thereafter, and in the immediate area, I heard a weapon discharge. In checking his .45 caliber pistol, our 'shotgun pilot' accidentally shot a hole in the right front seat floorboard of the jeep and right between his feet. Right after the .45 pistol was fired, a number of our enlisted men came out in the street, one of which had a hand-held M-60 machine gun and a bandoleer of ammo draped around his neck. My first instinct was to look for cover but on second thought, I rushed to the gunner to make sure he didn't hurt anyone. I guess you had to be there to appreciate the delayed humor of the situation that was enjoyed by most everyone. To say the least, our party was talked about for days, but future such events were discouraged by our leadership.

IN-COUNTRY R&R

I have already stated the fact that even though our area support mission took our Dustoff crews into many hazardous areas, we still had it much better than the aviation units that were assigned directly to our field forces. Our attitude was work hard when required, but always strive to make the situation as good as possible.

Along this line, our Commander, Colonel Madrano, authorized an in-country, three-day R&R (rest and relaxation) for our fight crews when possible. The R&R area would be the South Vietnam city of Da Lat, a beautiful mountainous area located west/southwest of the coastal city of Nha Trang. I would be going to Da Lat with one of our senior Majors.

Our crew flew from Qui Nhon into Da Lat, turned the aircraft over to the departing crew and checked into the Da Lat Palace Hotel. Being in the mountains, Da Lat was quite cool, a pleasant change from Qui Nhon.

On our second day, we rented a taxi to take us to the local zoo, located about five miles outside the city. We had been told that the area was safe and that we should have no trouble on our sightseeing trip. Upon arrival at the zoo, it seemed a bit peculiar that there was no gatekeeper and we were the only visitors. There was a large tiger, some monkeys, and different kinds of birds with the atmosphere being beautiful, but a bit eerie. There was also a beautiful waterfall of which I had pictures of, but have since lost or misplaced in my numerous moves.

After a couple of hours, we returned to Da Lat with no problems. It wasn't too long after our R&R to Da Lat that the city was placed off limits. The reason being that a number of U.S. engineer troops had been wounded and/or killed while improving a road just outside of the city. I was told later that the enemy attack had occurred on the very same road that we had travelled to and from the zoo.

One of the places that my eldest son, Britt, and I visited during a recent trip to Vietnam was Da Lat. It is still a beautiful city and received little or no damage as a result of the war. We did not stay in the Da Lat Palace Hotel but chose a smaller hotel nearer the center of the city. My son and I both enjoyed the people and the city, just like my visit in 1965.

BACK TO FLYING DUSTOFF MISSIONS

Taking enemy fire and actually getting the aircraft damaged was an interesting topic. It almost seemed that on reportedly insecure missions when you expected to take fire and/or hits, you didn't. And on missions that were called in as secure, you had better be on your toes. I will now address some facts and loose statistics concerning this subject.

I was taught and always believed that evasive flying into and out of a pickup site most definitely decreased the chances of taking fire and/or receiving hits. Flying fast and evasively coming out of an area was more restricted due to the fact that with on-board patients, your gross weight had increased reducing your ability to gain airspeed rapidly. My crews and I seemed to always take more hits while loading patients or while exiting the pickup site. Gunship escort, when available, was normally requested on insecure missions only. Their presence in the area was always a plus and usually negated and/or reduced enemy fire.

Another fact that was prevalent was that very seldom did we take fire or hits while flying missions for the Korean troops, either the ROK Tigers or the White Horse Division. Word had it that the ground commanders of both units were told by their superiors, "Don't get Dustoff aircraft shot up." They didn't, and we surely appreciated that fact. It always seemed that they extended their pickup site perimeters a lot more than some of the other units that we supported.

When flying Dustoff field pickups for the Koreans, we would always have a Korean interpreter on board our aircraft. He took a lot of pride in informing us that even though we may be evacuating gunshot wounds, he would say before landing, "Area safe, guide stand up in LZ." That was always comforting, also.

As they say, "There is always an exception to any rule or theory." The exception to my tactical evasive flying theory was none other than Captain Tom Osborne, our two platoons Aircraft Maintenance officer. Since we were both ACs, we did not fly much together, but when we did, he would be designated the AC since he was a Captain and I was a Lieutenant. His flight profile for all missions, regardless of the reported enemy activity, was normal approaches and normal takeoffs. Even though I was uncomfortable with Tom's flying technique, I must admit that we never took any hits while flying together.

I have two theories about his flying technique. One, being the Maintenance Officer, I know that he never wanted to overstress the aircraft, regardless of the fact that he sometimes overstressed me. Secondly, when and if we were ever shot at while Tom was flying, I just know that the enemy was always shooting way ahead of us, especially on approaches and exits from the pickup sites.

As I remember, the only hit he took on that first tour was while flying around 1000 to 1500 feet on a cross-country mission. Regardless of our different approach to flying combat missions, Tom Osborne was and still is one of my favorite friends.

As our first year tour progressed, we continued to receive a few additional aviators, both MSC and Warrant Officers. Just as it had been when we first arrived in Vietnam, most were right out of flight school but very willing to fly and learn as much as possible, as quickly as possible.

Not long after we arrived, Lt. Freddie Long and I were flying together on a field pickup mission. I told him to monitor the controls while I executed a high speed, low level approach into the pickup site. He said, "OK."

There was a long and wide open area on our selected entry route so I got on the deck, well away from the smoke marking the pickup site. While on the deck, and about half-way to the popped smoke, flying at 100 knots, a very large, leafless, grey tree appeared right in front of the aircraft. I banked right, just missing the tree limbs.

I said, "Fred, did you see that tree?"

He said, "Yes, and I figured you saw it, too."

We both laughed and made the pickup without incident. You will hear more about Fred later.

SUPPORTING THE LRRPs

Many of our Dustoff missions were exciting but there were two types that you could be sure would fit the category. The first was when you got a call that a LRRP (Long Range Recon Patrol) team had been wounded and was on the run. The main mission of LRRP teams numbering around eight or nine personnel, was to find the enemy, report, but not engage. The problem was the 'not engage' part. That was sometimes flat impossible. When it happened, the team was almost always outnumbered, in trouble, and for survival, had to run. The rule for us was that we were only supposed to respond to LRRP requests if they did, in fact, have wounded.

My rule and the rule of the vast majority of my fellow aviators was that we didn't question whether or not they had someone wounded, we just went to get them out of harm's way. I always felt that when they called and if they were on the run and we didn't get them out quickly, they would soon have someone wounded and/or killed.

The LRRPs were also famous for not wanting to pop smoke (daytime) or use what we considered adequate lighting (nighttime) at night to mark their position. They preferred to use a mirror during the day and maybe a cigarette lighter at night. I also understood their concern for secrecy and never questioned their methods.

When you got everyone on board the aircraft and the flight medic reported that no one had any visible sign of a wound, I would ask, "Which one of your fellows has heat exhaustion or a high fever?" The question seemed to always get a few smiles.

The other guaranteed touchy mission was the one that was called in as secure, but when you got radio contact with the ground radio operator, he only wanted to whisper his transmissions. That fact always caught my attention. Jokingly, I would sometimes whisper back, only to be asked, "Dustoff, why are you whispering on the radio?" I would reply, "Because you are whispering and I don't want to give your position away to the bad guys." Dead silence would follow.

R&R/BANGKOK

I was allowed to take two one week out-of-country R&Rs during my first tour in Vietnam. I chose to go to Bangkok with one of my unit buddies. We both enjoyed golf and had been told that Bangkok had one or more golf courses that we could play. We were also told to take as many cartons of Salem cigarettes as we could carry, contact a Mr. Porn, and he would take care of us during our stay. Mr. Porn? Now how is that for your future guide!

Upon our arrival, he picked us up at the airport and asked, "What do you two want do to?"

We said, "Play golf."

He said OK, and proceeded to take us to a nearby golf course. The interesting thing about this course was that it played through and around a horse racetrack. In fact, you sometimes had to delay your shot as the horses passed by. The caddies were all female and could find your ball (golf balls) even in the muddy canals, called clongs. Golf was both different in Bangkok and fun.

Mr. Porn was waiting for us when we finished playing golf and asked, "Would you now like to go for a massage and steam bath?"

We replied with, "That would be nice."

At the massage parlor, we were taken into a room with a large, see-through window. Soon a number of ladies appeared on the other side of the glass, all wearing numbers.

Mr. Porn then said, "Fellows, select your massage therapist."

We did, and he said he would be back later to take us to our hotel. I finished my massage and steam bath and returned to the parlor where Mr. Porn was waiting. A few minutes passed and Mr. Porn said he would go and check on my buddy. Returning, he said that my friend would be awhile longer and that he would go ahead and take me to the hotel. I didn't see my buddy for a couple of days, but Mr. Porn said he was doing fine. We both enjoyed our week in Bangkok and returned to Vietnam fully relaxed and refreshed.

AN UNFORTUNATE INCIDENT

Performing your duty in a combat situation, though often times a bit dangerous, was expected. I always felt that if I neglected such duties, someone else would have to take my place. I'm very proud to write that seeing such neglect in any of my fellow crewmembers was practically non-existent. But there was one occasion where I did observe a neglect of personal duty by one of my fellow aviators.

This particular individual joined our unit around the eighth or ninth month of my tour. Early on, it was noticed that the individual was grounded quite frequently due to certain medical problems. Later, I was told that the individual started having fainting spells. I initially felt badly for the person until one day while looking out my Quonset hut screen windows, I observed the following.

He was standing by our Herman Nelson generator, which supplied power for our air conditioning, seemingly ready to crank the unit. Prior to taking hold and turning the handle, I saw him look around to see if anyone was observing him. Not seeing anyone, he then fell to the ground, as if to faint. After seeing this and thinking about it for a short period of time, I reported the incident to one of my superiors. Not long afterwards, the individual was permanently grounded and placed in a non-flying assignment.

Was I a snitch? I don't think so, because safety wise, I know the right thing happened. I later learned that the aforementioned individual was one of the honor graduates in his flight class. Again, I am not one to judge, but in this particular case, I felt that an individual with these kind of problems would most likely jeopardize the safety of his other crew members and that he should not be flying. Later, I will write about one of our other pilots who often displayed a stressed, fearful nature, but always performed his missions successfully and with 100% effort.

R&R/TAIPAI, TAIWAN

My second out-of-country R&R was granted around the ninth month of my twelve month tour. I enjoyed Taipei, but as usual, a pleasant snafu occurred. When I reported to the Taipei airport to return to Vietnam, I was told, along with a number of others, that there was a charter aircraft dispute and we would not be scheduled to leave for three more days. I was told that my unit would be notified and asked if I needed any additional money for the extra stay. I naturally said yes to the money question, given $150.00, and instructed to return to the airport in three days. Talk about a bargain.

Due to the fact that instead of being flown from Taipei, Taiwan to Qui Nhon, I was flown to Pleiku, Vietnam, the location of our 4th Platoon, 498th Air Ambulance Company.

Naturally, my unit in Qui Nhon had not been notified by the military personnel in Taipei of the additional stay and I was being carried as AWOL (Absent Without Leave).

When I got to Qui Nhon the following day, I explained the situation, was only partially believed, but still had the balls to ask, "Why wasn't I being carried as missing in action?" No one laughed.

I have chosen not to write about and dwell on the many sad occurrences that took place during my two years of flying Dustoff Missions in Vietnam, but I do want to relate one other story that had a very strong impact on the way I approached all of missions.

Even though I spent very little time on the ground in what was considered hostile territory, it didn't take me long to figure out and understand that enemy land mines were probably the most feared weapon by our soldiers. To get seriously wounded or killed and not be able to confront one's enemy had to be very frustrating, thus what I consider to be one of the most meaningful and courageous acts that I ever witnessed. The mission came in as an urgent request to evacuate three U.S. land mine casualties from an insecure area. My crew and I responded immediately and were informed that our gunship support was already at the pickup site area. Upon arrival, we received the tactical situation, confirmed the number and condition of the casualties, and requested smoke to make the LZ. The casualties were located along a tree line and our approach would be made low level over flat, open terrain. Our exit would be made over the same general direction from which we came, if no fire was received on our approach into the area. We landed, the three patients were quickly loaded, and we began our exit. I informed the gunships that we would remain low level for two to three hundred meters and then execute a cyclic climb to altitude. Receiving no fire and reaching a safe altitude, I turned the controls over to my co-pilot. As I looked back into the cabin/cargo area where our flight medic and crew chief were treating the patients, this is what I saw. One of the injured soldiers looking at me gave 'thumbs up' with one of his hands. I could also see that he was missing one of his feet. What an attitude! So, you can understand why I and my flight crews always were adamant about doing everything that we could to get our sick and wounded out of further harm's way and to one of our medical treatment facilities. Our field troops were so brave.

FINAL DAYS

In June and July, 1966, we continued to receive more replacement personnel, to include MSC aviators, Warrant Officer aviators, and Enlisted personnel. We, in Qui Nhon, were also being told that some of our MSC aviators in Na Trang and Pleiku were receiving their port calls to return to the U.S.A. This was welcome news since we felt that our port calls would be coming soon.

Right about this time, a couple of our flight platoon leaders had been relieved due to the fact that they had been caught transporting some off-duty female nurses on a beach party trip to an outlying location. Luck would have it that my flight leader was one of those relieved and was replaced with an individual that I would really grow to dislike in a very short period of time.

My new 'leader' quickly became known as a special projects promoter, supposedly geared to improving our unit area beautification. In actuality, his efforts were to make it appear that he was too busy with the special projects to fly his normal duty roster periods. As previously stated, I had no problem with a person not flying missions whose attitude and heart were not going to be 100% committed. My problem was that I, and some of my fellow aviators, still did not have port calls and had already been responsible with making improvements to the unit area during our previous time in Qui Nhon. A confrontation was inevitable. Flying 1st up, and returning from a mission, I was walking back to my hooch to take care of a few personal matters. As I was approaching my living quarters, I observed one of my fellow aviators mixing cement. When I asked Fred what he was doing, he stated that he was mixing cement/mortar for our new sidewalks. I proceeded on into my hooch.

After taking care of my personal matters, I decided to take a siesta prior to our next missions. I was suddenly startled by someone lifting and dropping the foot end of my bed. Looking up out of my semi-sleep status, I saw none other than our new 'special projects officer', my new flight leader.

He said to me, "Covington, why aren't you outside assisting in the pouring of our new sidewalks?" I quickly informed him that there was no way in hell that I was going to assist anyone in the pouring of sidewalks or any other special projects he may have in mind. Realizing that I was really pissed, he left. I continued my nap. My attitude was in no way in disrespect for any of my fellow aviators who were new in-country and had very little choice in the matter. It had everything to do with the fact that my tour of duty (one year) was already complete and the only reason that I, and a few other of my fellow aviators, were still in Qui Nhon was because our port calls had not arrived.

Two things happened as a result of my encounter with our 'special projects officer'. One, good and one, a bit distasteful. The good one was that my former flight leader got wind of the incident and informed my new flight leader to leave me alone or he would kick his ass. The distasteful result was that my new flight leader informed me that I would be going to Tuy Hoa on a field standby until my port call arrived.

My initial feelings were that this is not a good way to spend your last days in Vietnam, especially since I had served my normal one year tour and was supposed to be on my way home. In retrospect, it was good to get away from my new flight leader because there is no telling just how much trouble I would have gotten into had I remained in Qui Nhon. As a result of this episode concerning sidewalk construction, I nicknamed my fellow aviator, Fred Long, 'Mortar Forker #1" and asked him to call me 'Mortar Forker #2'. Those nicknames have stuck to this day.

The next morning, my crew and I departed for our field standby at Tuy Hoa. My co-pilot would be Lt. Ike Gray, one of our relatively new pilots of whom I have written before. We would be supporting the 101st Airborne, the ARVN, and the Korean Whitehorse Division.

I had flown between five to ten missions with Ike and felt that on previous occasions, he had displayed a bit of additional nervousness. But I also remembered that I probably acted the same way my first month in Vietnam. I also realized that even though I wasn't in the best frame of mind for this field standby, I could and should not let it affect my attitude or performance during this period.

All went well on our missions and on the third day, I received word that another aircraft commander was on the way to Tuy Hoa to replace me. My port call had arrived.

The AC and crew chief arrived, I said goodbye to Ike, my crew chief and flight medic and the other crew chief, and I departed for Qui Nhon. I decided that instead of flying up the coastline to Qui Nhon, we would take an inland route.

On the way back to Qui Nhon, we received word that a Special Forces Camp had a patient to be evacuated to the 85th Evac. The patient supposedly had heat exhaustion. My crew chief and I made the pickup with no problem and to this day, I suspect that the Special Forces Troop was not sick in any way, but was on his way to R&R. Such is war.

OTHER MEMORIES BEFORE LEAVING QUI NHON

Before relating the memorable departure from Qui Nhon, I would like to relate a few stories about individuals that have stuck with me for all these years since serving in Vietnam. And even though the majority of my fellow unit personnel and friends were very special to me and to be sure, we had some very meaningful and exciting events happen to us, these next individuals and some memories about them have never been forgotten.

Lieutenants Frank Alverson and Jim Vance, both Dragon Gunship pilots, will always hold a special place and tremendous respect in my heart. They, along with a large number of other gunship pilots, did so much to protect our Dustoff Crews so we could be effective and successful in completing our medical evacuation missions.

Lt. Vance (and I say this with the utmost respect) was trained to kill the enemy. I had no problem with his killer attitude because I quickly realized that was his job. I speak of this because our Dustoff missions were so different, but yet we needed Jim and his crews' support to assist us in saving lives.

Another point about our totally different approach to the war was the fact that early on in my second tour in Vietnam (July 1968 – July 1969), I began to realize that our field soldiers, along with the ARVN, Koreans, Australians and other allies, were not being allowed to actually win the war. We would be allowed to win battles, but then vacate the area, only to have the Viet Cong and NVA move right back in to the same areas that had been won. The war had turned much more political than militarily oriented.

I write about this because I always felt that regardless of the politics and/or military decisions that were being made, our Dustoff mission of saving lives was always very worthwhile. To put it mildly, I was thankful that I was a Dustoff pilot. That feeling in no way detracts from the utmost respect I had for Lt. Vance, Lt. Alverson, their comrades and crews, and all of our ground troops that served in Vietnam.

I was not involved in this mission, but while flying gunship coverage, Captain Alverson took a round in his leg, severing his femoral artery. He was immediately taken to a medical facility where both his leg and life were saved. Another friend of mine, Lieutenant John "Pepe" LaCourse, a gunship pilot, received a similar wound to the leg. I learned about this while between tours and stationed at Ft. Sam Houston, Texas.

I immediately went to visit John who was in the Brook Army Medical Center there in San Antonio. I will never forget how upbeat he remained even though he lost his leg. To me, John did a couple of remarkable things after his injury. He entered law school, graduated, and became a successful attorney in San Antonio. He also continued to play golf with a one or two handicap, better than myself and many, many others with two legs. Knowing John, neither of these accomplishments surprised me.

If you are wondering why I have specifically written about these three individuals, I'll explain.

Early in my first tour, Lt. Vance helped me develop an attitude of invincibility because that's how he appeared to me. His positive attitude actually rubbed off. It never crossed my mind, or I would not allow it to, that I would not successfully complete both of my Vietnam tours and return to my family and loved ones in the U.S.A. Sure, I could have been wrong, but I always believed that it was so much better to be positive.

As for Frank Alverson and John LaCourse, both demonstrated to me the fact that even though one might get severely wounded, with the right attitude lots can be accomplished. I will speak of Lt. Vance later on to show you a more humorous and playful side to his personality.

RURAL SOUTH VIETNAMESE PEOPLE

Generally speaking, the South Vietnamese people were humble and peaceful. Many of them were confronted with a very difficult and dangerous position during the war. On the one hand, they had to deal with the Viet Cong and the North Vietnam Communists and on the other, the South Vietnam Military and the Allied Forces. In an effort to protect their families, one should be able to understand that they were compelled to a very large degree to side with whomever was in power at the time in their local living areas. A great book by Jay Wurts entitled *When Heaven and Earth Changed Places* is a non-fiction story about a young Vietnamese girl who lived and survived in this difficult situation. She currently resides on our West Coast. This is a great book that vividly describes her life, her many difficult situations, and her survival. If you would like to get a better understanding of this aspect of the Vietnam War, I highly recommend that you read this book by Mr. Wurts. It most definitely gives a good view and more understanding of those that at some times sided with our enemy.

DEPARTING QUI NHON

Having flown my last mission, and being one of the last six 'original' members of the 498th Air Ambulance Company, it goes without saying that we were all ready to get the hell out of Vietnam. We were all told that we were on our own and would have to secure our own air transportation to Saigon to catch our flights to the U.S.A.

Our situation certainly brought back memories of our arrival one year earlier in Qui Nhon when we had no one to meet us and no place to stay. Back then, I was highly motivated to stay in Qui Nhon and not get on a Chinook bound for An Khe. But this time, I was even more motivated to find transportation and get to Saigon ASAP. I packed my things, said my goodbyes, and headed for airfield operations.

I was told that there was a transit Otter that would be going to Saigon shortly and had three available seats. I said, "Put me on the manifest and I will be back shortly with two of my friends."

I went back to our operations building to relay the information about the Otter flight and was told that there was also a C-119 that would be going a little later in the afternoon to Saigon. I told everyone that the Otter was leaving shortly and that I would be on-board. A couple of my mates laughed and asked if I knew that the Otter cruises at ninety knots that they would leave later on the C-119 and be in Saigon when I arrived. They also promised to have cocktails waiting upon my arrival in Saigon at the Red Bull Inn.

I later found out that the C-119 had a South Vietnamese crew, some pigs and chickens as cargo, and would be flying a low-level photo mission en route to Saigon. The bottom line was that my two other buddies and I made 'Happy Hour' that afternoon at the Red Bull Inn in Saigon. Our other buddies that chose to fly in the C-119 arrived later that evening worn out and not smelling very good.

We were hosted for a couple of nights by members of the 57th Medical Detachment (AA), the aeromedical unit known as the 'Original Dustoff' unit in Vietnam. Ironically, I would later be assigned to that unit on my second tour in Vietnam.

VIETNAM TO U.S.A.

Prior to leaving Saigon, I was told that I would be flying on a commercial jet that would land in Washington, D.C. I would be further booked on a Piedmont Airlines flight to Fayetteville, North Carolina, some 50 miles from Rockingham, North Carolina, my hometown. Rockingham was where both my wife's parents and my parents lived. That was also where my wife, Jenny, and my two children, Britt and Cindy, were living while I served in Vietnam. I was also told that upon arrival in D.C., I would have adequate time to notify my family of my arrival time in Fayetteville.

We departed Saigon during the night, which was normal for safety purposes. Upon liftoff, the aircraft passenger area erupted in loud and boisterous cheers. Not long after that, most of us were sound asleep, probably with smiles on our faces.

Arriving in D.C., I had three hours before my Piedmont flight to Fayetteville. I called both my wife, Jenny, and my parents, Ralph and Juanita Covington, to let them know of my expected arrival time in Fayetteville.

As we were taxiing up to the terminal in Fayetteville, I was able to look out the window and I noticed a fairly large number of folks waiting for everyone to depart the aircraft. Back then, we would use stairs to depart the aircraft and then walk to the terminal via the parking area. As I reached the bottom of the stairs, I thought I recognized one of the ramp personnel, As I got closer to him, he smiled and said, "Welcome home, Bill Covington. I'm Billy Beecham."

I shook his hand and we began talking about playing against each other in high school football. Billy was from Laurinburg, North Carolina and a star halfback on their football team. I had played quarterback for my hometown of Rockingham and we had played three years against each other. After talking with Billy for a couple of minutes, I began to hear some loud voices from the ramp area. About twenty people were waving at me and motioning for me to get my butt over to see them.

Billy said, "You better go or we both are going to be in real trouble."

As I approached my wife, my two children, my parents and other family friends I began to feel my eyes moisten up. I had not seen any of them for over one year and it dawned on me that I was finally home. God bless my family, my friends and my country. I think my dad was the only one that realized that Billy Beecham was someone that I knew and had possibly played some sport against either in high school or college. In fact, knowing my dad, he had probably spoken with Billy before my arrival to the airport.

HOMECOMING

I hugged, kissed and/or shook hands with everyone that had come to the airport to welcome me home. It was such a meaningful and beautiful feeling. My hometown of Rockingham was about fifty miles away. I was so happy to see everyone, especially my family, that I have no idea what we talked about on the way home.

Britt, my son, was now a little over four years old and seemed to remember me somewhat. But Cindy, my daughter, now almost two years old, had no idea who I was and naturally was a bit standoffish. I certainly understood. Jenny relayed to me that in an effort to help Britt and Cindy remember me, she would frequently show them my picture. It helped because it wasn't very long before I was getting lots of hugs and kisses from both of them.

I had rented a small, two-bedroom apartment for my family to stay in during my time away. When we arrived, I immediately noted a yellow ribbon tied around the tree in our front yard with, 'Welcome Home, Dad' attached. Again, tears came to my eyes and under my breath, I said, "Thank you, God." Since that time, I have probably listened to Tony Orlando and Dawn and others sing, 'Tie a Yellow Ribbon 'Round the Ole Oak Tree' so many times that I can recite the lyrics.

Since I had not been with my wife and two children for over a year, I remember that I was very content just sitting, watching, and listening to them talk and jabber (Cindy) about whatever. Yes, for sure, absence makes the heart grow fonder.

Naturally, everyone was very happy and thankful that I had returned from Vietnam both safe and sound. As for me, I had never thought that it would have been any other way. Yes, I had my moments of fear, but truly never doubted that if I didn't do anything really stupid, I would return home to my family, much the same way that I had left.

The more I have thought about my positive attitude, I now have even more understanding and empathy for those of my fellow comrades that didn't quite have the same state of mind. Fear and uneasiness is quite normal, but too much of either may lead to poor judgment or some other problem.

Prior to departing Vietnam, I had received two sets of orders. One was a promotion to Captain, which was very nice, especially the pay raise. A family of four could certainly use the money. I don't think I ever mentioned the main reason I took ROTC (Reserve Officers Training Corps) was to get the $27.00/month. That was a lot of money in 1960 for most everyone, especially a country boy from North Carolina. The other set of orders was my assignment to the 54th Medical Detachment (Air Ambulance), Ft. Benning, Georgia.

CHAPTER FIVE

SEPTEMBER, 1966 – DECEMBER, 1967

FT. BENNING, GEORGIA

As stated, my assignment orders were to the 54th Air Ambulance Medical Detachment at Ft. Benning, Georgia, the 'Home of the Infantry'. Three of my 498th Vietnam pilot buddies (Ed Haswell, Jerry Spruiell, and Roger Hula) were also assigned to the 54th.

Arriving and signing in to our unit at Ft. Benning, we learned that the detachment had six UH19 helicopters. Having flown UH1Ds in Vietnam, the UH19 was quite a letdown. Our primary mission was to provide area aeromedical support to Ft. Benning and one each helicopter crews to both the North Georgia Dahlonega and North Florida Eglin Ranger School Training sites.

The Florida site was located on the Eglin AFB complex at Field #7. Now, for those of you that aren't familiar with the UH19 helicopter, it is a big, ugly, underpowered, seven-cylinder aircraft designed to transport a maximum of one patient or passenger, plus a crew of three. Now, that is a bit of an exaggeration, but closer to the truth than not.

I actually took to the aircraft pretty quickly, was signed off by the unit IP (Instructor Pilot) and cleared for single-pilot operation. Since this book is primarily dedicated to my two tours in Vietnam, I will relate only a few stories about Ft. Benning that might interest you.

One of the checkout requirements for the UH19 helicopter was for me to perform some autorotations to the ground/pad with our IP on board. Since the UH19 had wheels, you could do a rolling type autorotation or one with minimum or practically no ground roll. The pads that we used for the touchdowns were relatively narrow and short, encouraging the minimum roll-type landing. I felt good about my landings and the IP signed me off as being good to go.

About a week later and after picking up an injured airborne trainee from Fryer DZ (drop zone) and transporting him to the local post hospital (Martin Army Hospital), I decided to do some more autorotations at the airfield.

After dropping off our flight medic, my crew chief Specialist Bullock and I proceeded to accomplish some autorotations. After three or four, the tower operator called and said that I needed to report to our unit operations officer ASAP. I figured that another mission had come in for me and my crew so I immediately hovered over to our operations, shut down the aircraft, and went inside.

Someone said, "Major Taylor wants to see you right now." I went inside Major Taylor's office and he immediately asked me why I was practicing solo pilot autorotations without the unit IP on board the aircraft.

My answer was, "He had already checked me out so what is the problem?"

He stated, "It's not allowed in accordance with our unit SOP (Standard Operating Procedure), so don't do it anymore." I said fine and was dismissed. Since we flew single-pilot on most of our missions and would most definitely not have an IP on board in case we had an engine failure, I never quite understood either the logic of such a rule nor the SOP. My take on the subject surely questions the army's decision to stop aotorotations to the ground during flight training. That decision had to be made due to money/costs and not to good common sense. What do you think?

In an effort to explain just how underpowered the UH19 was, I will relate a couple of facts. On a hot day, in order to transport one or two patients from a field location, I would have to have the crew chief remain at the pickup site while the flight medic and I transported the patient(s) to the hospital. Another example was when taking off from Yonah Mountain, North Georgia Ranger Training area, I would have to immediately fly down the mountainside to gain enough airspeed to fly the aircraft straight and level.

Lastly, while flying the aircraft in normal flight, you had to be extremely careful as to not enter a condition known as retreating blade stall. What this simply meant was that if you flew the aircraft too fast, the blades were not designed to handle the speed, consequently causing the retreating blade to stall, which could and would result in an inability to fly the aircraft, possibly resulting in an accident if not corrected immediately.

Why do I mention this flight restriction? Well, it almost caused me to lose a race with a 1957 Plymouth that some of our unit members had pitched in and bought so we would have transportation while on field standby at the Ranger Training Site in Northwest Florida. The race was between me flying the aircraft, and my unit pilot buddy, Phil Livermore, who was driving the 1957 Plymouth from Ft. Benning to the Florida Ranger Training Site. As I remember, I won the race by about 30 minutes. It was close.

Both of our field standbys were interesting and enjoyable duty. At the Mountain Ranger Training in North Georgia, I got to do a bit of trout fishing. As for excitement, I was shown how to rappel off of the boards and also met the challenge on both night and day medevacs off of Yonah Mountain. I've already spoken of how interesting those missions could be.

From my perspective, the Mountain Ranger Training was geared to teach the potential graduates a number of skills that could or would be needed in the accomplishment of some of their assigned missions. On the other hand, I saw the final phase of training in North Florida to be more of a test of endurance. Sure, there were some skills to be learned, but basically this phase was to push the candidates to the brink of just what they could withstand physically.

I am not sure but I think this was the phase that eliminated the highest percentage of trainees. It was extremely rough, and from my observation standpoint, the toughest training that I had observed thus far in my service career. That fact remains to this day. Anyone that wears the Ranger Tab has every right to be extremely proud of such an accomplishment.

While on standby at the Florida Ranger Camp, I had the privilege of meeting and talking with a number of the cadre and especially their leader, LTC Charles Beckwith. He was very inspirational and personified the highest degree of courage and dedication of military service on behalf of our country.

He would encourage my crew and I to take some time off when there was a training lull, but he was quick to suggest that we not go to the Eglin Beach Officer's Club. He explained that some of his officer cadre had gotten a little upset with someone at the club, resulting in said individual being tossed through a plate glass window. He smiled and said, "We Rangers are barred from the club until further notice."

I had been assigned to the 54th Air Ambulance Detachment for around six months when the unit received word that it would be deployed shortly for Vietnam. Those of us that had recently returned would be assigned to an assault platoon and would receive six CH34s to fly our aeromedical mission. The CH34 would be a big step up from the UH19 in that it was larger and a lot more powerful. We were also told that on occasion, when the aircraft were available, we would be allowed to fly some UH1Ds. That was also great news.

I, along with a few other unit pilots, crew chiefs, and flight medics – were alerted that we would be accompanying a large air assault contingent out of Ft. Benning to fly to Ft. Bragg, North Carolina to participate in a big air assault exercise with the 82nd Airborne. Our medical personnel would be flying UH1Ds and performing the aeromedical evacuation mission. We expected to be in North Carolina for seven to ten days. The few aeromedical missions that we flew were quite normal with no undue circumstances. I will relate a couple of missions that I flew that I consider of a training nature and I'll just let it go at that.

The first involved doing a favor for a very dear high school friend of mine. Mr. LeGrand Land, though not a high school classmate and quite a bit older, had been very nice to me and some of my baseball teammates while I was in high school. He owned a dairy farm and quite a bit more land just outside of Hamlet, North Carolina. He would take me and some of my friends, on occasion, to his dairy farm and treat us to the best chocolate milk that you can imagine. He would also take one of my best friends, Jerry Goodman, and me to Charlotte, North Carolina before our baseball season to pick out our team baseball bats.

Well, due to the fact that my hometown of Rockingham was only fifteen miles from Camp McCall, our assault staging area for the exercise, I got permission to go and visit my parents for one overnight. On this visit, I also ran into Mr. Legrand Land. One of the things that came up in our conversation was the fact that he had a large pecan orchard and that the pecans had not been falling off the trees as fast as they normally would. I commented that I bet I could change that fact with a helicopter. He happily agreed and the rest is history.

I had already been alerted that the aeromedical community was about to be issued aircraft hoists and I figured such a mission would give me a bit of a head start in that type of low-level training. You be the judge.

Another similar incident occurred having to do with collecting one of my favorite all-time jackets, my one and only 'London Fog'. What happened was that on a visit to Ft. Bragg during the exercise and while staying in the BOQ (Bachelor's Officer's Quarters), I had left my jacket behind before returning to Camp McCall. On the day before leaving

Camp McCall for our return to Ft. Benning, I got permission to take a 'training flight' to Ft. Bragg.

Since there would be a problem in getting transportation from either the Ft. Bragg airfield or the medevac pad at Womack Army Hospital, I told the crew chief, who was flying as my co-pilot, that I would be landing near the BOQ, which was located right beside the PX. At that time, I told him that I would leave the aircraft running and I would quickly go inside the BOQ to retrieve my jacket. Though he looked a little concerned, he said, "O.K."

There was a parking lot that was mostly vacant right between the PX and the BOQ. I landed and went to get my jacket. There was about a 10-minute delay while the BOQ staff located my jacket. Upon returning to the helicopter, my crew chief stated that a couple of MPs (Military Police) who had stopped vehicle traffic in the area had asked what was going on. He said he told them we were picking up some important cargo and they seemed to have bought the story. We immediately vacated the area and proceeded to Camp McCall.

Before departing the main base of Ft. Bragg, I heard the Ft. Bragg tower request identification of aircraft that had landed in the PX parking lot. On second thought, I didn't hear that transmission. The remaining two days at Camp McCall was uneventful and our trip back to Ft. Benning went well.

While in the 54th, I was privileged to fly with and meet some truly outstanding individuals. Sadly, two of the young lieutenants, just out of helicopter flight training that had come to fly with us for a short period time, were later killed in Vietnam while flying Dustoff missions. Lieutenants Tom Chiminello and Jack Licte were these two individuals. May God rest their souls.

Lieutenant Phil Livermore was also severely wounded while flying Dustoff in Vietnam. He survived and successfully completed his military career in the MSC Corps. LTC Bob McWilliams was the deployable Commander of the 54th and was known as a leader who always looked after the well-being of his men and was admired by all.

Captain Pat Brady was the deployable Operation Officer of the 54th and would be returning to Vietnam for a second tour. As a member of the 54th in Vietnam, Pat was awarded the Medal of Honor for a series of extremely hazardous Dustoff missions flown in I Corp, South Vietnam. Pat later transferred out of the Army Medical Services Corps and became a General Officer.

CHAPTER SIX

JANUARY, 1968 – JULY, 1968

FT. SAM HOUSTON, TEXAS

Having returned from Vietnam for one year, some of us were offered the opportunity to attend the MSC Officers six-month Advanced Course. We were told that we could attend the course immediately or wait for another course beginning later on. My wife and I had previously talked about staying in or getting out of the military. I knew that if I stayed in, I would be returning to Vietnam. We were both OK with that.

Now, I am no genius, but I figured it was best to wait six or so months to attend the advanced course because I knew that upon graduation, I would immediately return to Vietnam. That would give me two years with my family instead of eighteen months. That's what I did.

I would like to take this opportunity to personally thank the entire staff and cadre of the MSC Officer Advanced Course, January through June, 1968. I think it quickly became very apparent to them that a large number of those attending, especially MSC aviators, would be returning to Vietnam upon graduation. They accepted such things as reduced attendance by such individuals on Friday afternoon.

They also accepted that if there was only one person on a given row to handle roll call and reporting that all were present on a given day, that was accepted. And most importantly, it was expected that everyone would graduate, but not necessarily with honors.

During the latter part of the course, I was asked to come to the Officer's Club Annex known as the 'Pit' to meet with LTC Arlie Price and LTC Dick Scott. They were designated to be the two commanding officers of our two Aeromedical Companies in Vietnam, the 45th in Long Binh and the 498th in Qui Nhon. LTC Scott would be commanding the 498th

and LTC Scott, the 45th. Both of these officers, along with myself, were original members of the 498th.

Since I had served my first tour with the 498th in II Corps, and was very familiar with the unit's area of responsibility, I was told that I would be assigned to the 498th.

CHAPTER SEVEN

JULY, 1968 – JULY, 1969

2ND TOUR – SOUTH VIETNAM

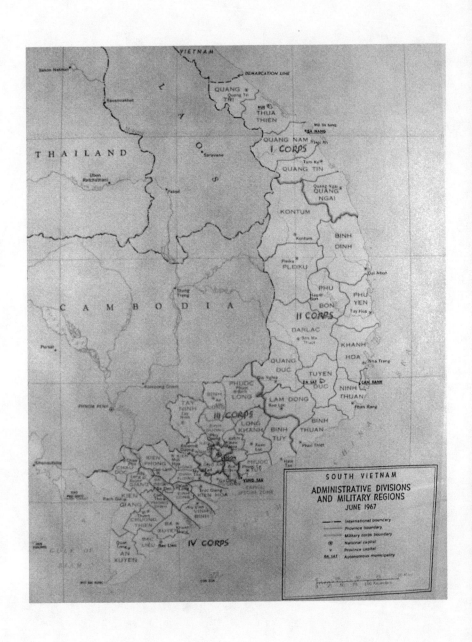

Upon graduation and saying goodbye to all my friends, my family and I departed San Antonio, Texas for my hometown of Rockingham, North Carolina. I would soon be off to my second tour in Vietnam. My wife and I were able to buy a nice three-bedroom home in Rockingham where my family could reside while I was away. My vacation time went quickly and I soon said goodbye.

I initially flew commercially to San Francisco and was told by the Army Liaison Office that I would later be bused to Travis AFB, just north of San Francisco for my flight to Vietnam. Since I would not be leaving Travis for three to four days, I was told that I could remain in the city for a couple of nights.

Being the baseball fan that I am and hearing that the Giants were in town, I decided to attend a game that night. Thank goodness that I had a flight jacket because as I had heard, the nights were quite cool at Candlestick Park. I don't remember which team won the game but Jimmy Wynn, the 'Toy Cannon', hit a towering home run out of the park. What power for such a little man.

Another very exciting and meaningful incident happened in San Francisco. No, I didn't go to Haight Ashbury in my Army uniform to see what the 'hippy' reaction would be. I must tell you though, that while wearing my uniform in San Francisco, I was never belittled or treated poorly by anyone.

In fact, having eaten and liking quite a bit of oriental food on my first tour in Vietnam, I decided to have dinner the next day in China Town. I was sitting at a table for two in uniform, facing the front door, when a black limousine pulled up and parked in front of the restaurant. A group of five or six people got out of the limo, entered the front door and were welcomed by one of the employees.

I immediately recognized one of the men as Mr. Tony Bennett. I had already ordered and had received my hot tea. Mr. Bennett and his group were taken to two large tables toward the back of the dining area and were seated. Not long after receiving my food, my waiter came over to me and informed me that Mr. Bennett would like to treat me to a bottle of wine. I graciously accepted. After finishing my dinner and most of the wine, I decided it would be only proper to thank Mr. Bennett personally.

Upon walking up to his table, he said, "I bet I know where you are either going to or coming from."

I replied, "Going."

And as I remember, he said something like, "Thank you for your service and good luck."

I thanked him for the wine and wished him and his friends a nice evening. Do you think if I would have asked him to sing 'I Left My Heart in San Francisco' he would have granted my request? Probably not. But the incident gave me a good feeling about beginning my second tour in Vietnam.

ARRIVAL IN SAIGON

Life has many unexpected surprises and upon arrival in Saigon, I was about to experience one of these.

Per my orders and expecting to be scheduled for a flight north to Qui Nhon and the 498th Air Ambulance Company, I was informed that I was being reassigned to the 45th Air Ambulance Company at nearby Long Binh. I figured that the 45th was short pilots, resulting in my reassignment. A driver from the 45th came to pick me up at the Repo Depot (Replacement Detachment) and we drove to the 45th Headquarters at Long Binh.

LTC Price, the Commander, welcomed me and proceeded to explain that the 45th was short a fixed-wing pilot and I was being assigned to fill the slot. What immediately came to mind was the fact that the 45th Air Ambulance Company was a Dustoff aeromedical evacuation unit with only UH1H helicopters assigned.

I was confused and in a somewhat pissed off frame of mind when I began to relate to Colonel Price that I came back to Vietnam to fly Dustoff missions and not to fly some fixed-wing aircraft. In a totally calm and quiet voice, a mannerism that I would see a lot more of in Colonel Price, he said, "Bill, let me further explain."

He went on to say that Jack Wofford, an MSC pilot friend of mine, was in Vung Tau flying the assigned fixed-wing Otter and he needed my assistance for awhile.

My reaction was, "An Otter?", as I immediately reflected on my last and only previous flight from Qui Nhon to Saigon some two years earlier to catch my flight back to the U.S.

Colonel Price went on to explain that the aircraft was attached to the 45th and being used to transport medical personnel and supplies throughout South Vietnam. Even though Jack Wofford was a good friend of mine and probably the best overall aviator that I had ever flown with, I still wasn't happy.

Realizing my state of mind, Colonel Price went on to say that in approximately one month, the 45th platoon leader at Vung Tau would be returning to the U.S. and I would take his job.

The platoon at Vung Tau had six UH1H helicopters and the unit had the area aeromedical support mission plus a field standby with the Australians at a place called Nui Dat. He also said that my Otter flying would cease just as soon as he was able to get some additional fixed wing aviators.

He went on to say that Vung Tau was located on the beach and quite a nice place to be stationed to get my combat command time. A bit of guilt about suddenly getting such a choice assignment crept into my mind, but not to worry, things can change in a hurry in a combat zone.

VUNG TAU

After spending a couple of days in Long Binh in-processing and meeting a number of the other unit personnel, I was ready to depart for Vung tau.

The 45th had the headquarters, operations, supply, maintenance, and two flight platoons located at Long Binh. Thirteen UH1H helicopters were authorized. Another platoon consisting of six UH1H were located to the northwest at a place called Lai Khe. As stated before, my new platoon assignment was at Vung Tau. Our 45th company mission was area support for the III Corp area and some of IV Corp to include a number of field standbys dispersed through the two areas. All of the 45th UH1Hs were equipped with hoists.

Upon arrival via a 45th Long Binh UH1H, I was met by my friend, Jack Wofford, at the platoon helipad at Vung Tau, who said, "Welcome, Bill Covington. I have something to show you."

Knowing Jack like I did, I still had no idea what kind of surprise I had in store. Not long after leaving the helipad in a unit truck, we entered what appeared to be a salvage storage yard. After winding through the area for awhile, Jack stopped the vehicle and pointed at what looked like a very damaged boat perched up on an eight-foot platform.

He said to me, "We are going to sail that boat in the South China Sea before we leave Vietnam." My thought was that to do so, we would definitely have to extend our one-year tour commitment.

I laughed and said, "Jack, let's go have a beer or two so I can get in a better frame of mind to believe the next thing that you tell me." More about the boat later.

Jack, being the Platoon IP in both the Otter and the UH1H, gave me a checkout and we began to fly missions. Our call sign for the Otter, so appropriately made, was 'Medicare 278'.

The Otter was a very consistent fixed wing, single-engine aircraft. It climbed at ninety knots, cruised at ninety knots, and descended at ninety knots. Since we were definitely not going to break any sound barriers, we elected to frequently continue missions at night in an attempt to complete them on a somewhat timely basis. I can remember flying into Da Nang at sundown, refueling to continue to Quang Tri, and being begged by one of my flight school classmates Doug Keithly to wait until morning to continue.

He would say, "Bill, our survival chances at night aren't very good if that Spartan rebuilt engine decides to quit on you." Doug was assigned to an Otter Company and was stationed in Da Nang. His unit had undoubtedly had a number of daytime engine failures and flew night missions only if absolutely necessary.

It didn't dawn on me just how serious Doug was until he gave me a two-barreled derringer with some ammo and said, "This is for you, Jack, and your crew chief and not the NVA if you go down." I understood. Maybe we were just lucky, but we never had an engine failure, day or night.

But, there are other types of failures. Jack and I had been invited to attend a 498th unit party at Qui Nhon on our way back to Vung Tau on one of our missions up north. We were scheduled to land at the Qui Nhon airfield around 1800 hours and would be picked up by one of the 498th helicopters. The 498th was no longer located on the airfield but had its own heliport in the valley just outside of Qui Nhon.

After refueling the Otter for the next morning's flight back to Vung Tau, and walking away from the aircraft, we heard a shot. Our crew chief, while clearing his M-16 rifle inside the aircraft, accidently discharged his weapon, resulting in holes in two of the three fuselage fuel tanks. After saving as much of the fuel as possible, we spent most of the night dismantling the cabin floor to determine the damage prior to departing for Vung Tau the next day.

No, we did not attend the 498th party and no, we did not press any charges against our Crew Chief. Sure, he had been told and knew that he should never clear his weapon inside the aircraft and that he had made a careless mistake. But he was young and very dependable in so many other ways, so we gave him a break. The results were that he continued to be very dedicated and dependable and never made another mistake.

I quickly learned that Jack had made quite a few friends outside of Vung Tau. This became apparent when were returning to Vung Tau with an empty Otter. On our refueling stops at certain places, we would pick up some supplies. It's amazing what it takes to rebuild a tri-maran with very extensive damage. It's also amazing just what one could get with a few enemy weapons. It was not uncommon for our Dustoff crews to be asked to transport captured enemy weapons on some of our missions with no guidance as to where or how to dispose of such weapons.

Finally, we received two additional fixed wing aviators to assist Jack, and I was able to dedicate my full attention to my new job as the Dustoff Flight Platoon Leader.

When I had first arrived at Vung Tau to fly the Otter, I learned that at Headquarters, the 45th was using the Vung Tau Platoon as the unit of assignment for short-time personnel (two months or less) that would soon be returning to the states.

After awhile, upon assuming command of the platoon, we began to get a number of pilots from the States right out of flight school. Our mission at the time was area support, a field standby with the Australians and an occasional field standby at Phan Thiet. Normally, none of these missions offered very much combat flying experience.

I was also informed that after two to three months, these new, inexperienced aviators would be transferred to other assignments within the 45th. Knowing that the flying with the two platoons at Long Binh and the 4th Platoon at Lai Khe was much more hazardous than what we were doing, concerned me on behalf of these new, inexperienced pilots.

So I made the request to Long Binh Operations that we needed one or two more field standbys, preferably in the Mekong Delta, which would afford some better flying experience for the new pilots. Nothing happened, so I continued to send my request to the 45th Operations Officer, Mike Trader. I knew and liked Mike and felt that he had the same regard for me. I was unaware of the fact that, for whatever the reason, he was under quite a bit of stress at Long Binh.

It wasn't long before I received a call from Mike. He said, "OK, Bill, here are your missions beginning tomorrow and until further notice."

In addition to our 1st up area support aircraft at Vung Tau and our normal field standby at Nui Dat, he assigned us permanent field standbys at both Phan Thiet and Dong Tam, which was in the Mekong Delta.

We only had ten pilots at the time, which meant that eight out of ten would be on duty on a daily basis, 24 hours a day. I welcomed this increase and our platoon quickly began to lead the company in missions flown and patients evacuated. Our new pilots and crews were getting lots of combat experience very rapidly. That was just what they needed and I was very pleased and proud of all of our personnel. Up until this time, I had felt embarrassed about being assigned to Vung Tau. In fact, anytime I had a friend come and visit me, I always insisted on buying any dinners and drinks involved.

THE AUSTRALIANS

The Aussies at Nui Dat were great soldiers and individuals and were a pleasure to support on our field standbys. When needed, they would always supply an additional flight medic or gunner. As you probably know, they also love their beer (piss). It was always a challenge to gracefully turn them down when they wanted me and my crew to have a drink with them at night. Our policy was no drinking while on duty and 'X' hours before going on duty. ('X' had a bit of a sliding scale as you can imagine.)

In an effort to get you to tilt one, they would say such things as, "We don't have anyone on patrol in the field tonight."

And I would always respond with, "Yes, but we are the backup crew for our 1st up aircraft back at Vung Tau."

They would honor my answer but it was not uncommon to find a case of Fosters or Victorian Bitters in our aircraft before departing for Vung Tau, ending our field standby. Again, great soldiers and great people.

When I told some of the Aussies that I would be going to Sydney on R&R in a couple of weeks, their eyes lit up and they began to tell me what a great time I was going to have. Even knowing that I was married with a family, they couldn't resist describing in detail just how beautiful and nice their 'birds' (women) were. Some of them even went on to say that some of their women seemed to have a special liking for 'yanks' (Americans). The only thing that could explain their lack of jealously for such information was the fact that some of the Aussies preferred drinking their 'piss' just as much as paying attention to their ladies. I have no facts to back up my point, just a hunch on the subject.

They suggested that I get a room in the area known as King's Cross and a few of them insisted that I visit their families and bring back some proof of the visits. I was emphatically informed that returning with no evidence of the family visits would most likely result in my crews and me receiving some 'friendly fire' on one of my future Dustoff missions. I assured them that I would make every attempt to make the visits. I did just that and had a great time visiting the families.

Again, the Aussies are the most hospitable people that I have ever met, and I have met a lot of nice people from different cultures and backgrounds.

Let me relate an incident that occurred prior to my R&R to Australia, but is related to the trip.

One of our MSC Dustoff pilots from a sister unit had received a gunshot wound to his leg/thigh area which required quite a number of surgical stitches to close the wound after debridement. I received word that he was being allowed to come to Vung Tau to recover in the 36th Evacuation hospital. On one of my visits to see him, he informed me that he really needed to have a night out on the town.

I said, "No problem. Just get the head nurse's permission."

As I mentioned before, I had somewhat of a guilt complex about being assigned to Vung Tau. After all, it was used as an in-country R&R center. When anyone visited, I always tried to do anything that I could to make their stay as nice as possible. That always included free food and drinks.

The head nurse informed me that a night on the town for my friend was no problem, but that I was responsible for his well-being. No problem, right?

urning to the hospital the morning after our night on the
nd told me that at least one-half of the stitches in his leg
d needed to be placed. I told him he was on his own to get
de, but in no circumstances could he allow the head nurse
knowledge of the incident. He was taken care of and I thought all was well until I saw the head nurse about a week later.

She smiled and asked me, "Bill, how is your friend's leg doing?" I thought that was cool and knew that if she ever needed a favor, I would comply.

It was later on when my previously wounded friend and I went to Sydney together. We stayed at King's Cross and had a great time. His leg had healed and he received no more noticeable injuries on the trip. We got an additional bonus on our return trip to Vietnam in that we lost an engine en route and got to spend two additional days in Darwin, Australia.

The only problem was that the average temperature in Sydney was between 60 to 70 degrees, with Darwin's being around 90 to 100 degrees, just like Vietnam. It was hot, hot, hot. But, the days counted on our tours so we had no complaints.

One more quick story before moving on to some serious flying.

As stated earlier, the majority of our Dustoff pilots were young Warrant officers. On my initial field standby to Nui Dat to fly for the Australians and prior to becoming the Flight Platoon Leader, I was paired with WO1 Wright. Due to the fact that he had already been in-country for at least ten months, he was designated as the Aircraft Commander. He informed me that he would initially fly the UH1H and we took off low-level across the Vung Tau Bay.

It wasn't very long before a number of seagulls in our flight path rose from the water with one of them striking the helicopter windscreen. It appeared to startle WO1 Wright more than me since I quickly observed that no damage had been done, there was just a lot of blood, guts and feathers on the windscreen. He immediately ascended, not saying a word. Not too long after the incident, the word must have gotten out, probably via our on-board crew chief, and I started hearing him being referred to as Mr. Wrong instead of Mr. Wright. All is fair in love and war.

MEKONG DELTA

It was not uncommon, while on standby in the Mekong Delta, to get an identical mission request along with one of our platoons located in the

Long Binh area. This would normally happen when the pickup site was at or near a midpoint between our two locations.

On one particular night, the following happened to me and my standby crew.

We arrived first at the site and were told that there were numerous casualties that were disbursed throughout the area. We were also told that there was enemy fire in the area, precluding consolidating the patients in one place.

I understood the situation and informed the ground radio man that we would begin policing up the patients. As we hovered around the area with both our landing and search lights on, we didn't appear to take any enemy fire. I have no explanation for that fact since we were picking up gunshot wounds, but I was very thankful. We took no hits and once we had our maximum load of patients, we departed the area en route to the hospital.

As we departed, the Dustoff crew from Long Binh were arriving. Cpt. Fred Grates, the AC on the arriving Dustoff, asked me for a brief on the situation. I informed him of the requirement to hover around the area in order to find and pickup the remaining patients. When asked about enemy fire, I stated that we had received none and that his pickups should be a 'piece of cake'.

The fact of the matter was that during their hovering and pickups, they did receive enemy fire and some hits, but none critical to the point of precluding the remaining patient pickups. To me, the only feasible explanation was that Charlie/Viet Cong had seen enough of the 'glowing light show' and figured no Dustoff crew would be foolish enough to attempt such an action again, thus the decision to open fire. Such is war.

Now, for one of my very favorite stories about another field standby in the Mekong Delta. You could appreciate it more if you could have been there, but let me give it a shot.

It was customary to arrive at Dong Tam, one of our Mekong Delta standbys, around 0900 hours. We would receive a briefing from our on-station standby crew and they would be released to return to Vung Tau.

Just before arrival, we received a radio call from our outdoing crew that they were on a mission and had another pickup for us to make. I rogered the transmission, requested pickup coordinates, and proceeded to the pickup site. Both of our crews flew for approximately two hours and I felt it was OK to release the previous crew to return to Vung Tau. Oh yes, I was the Flight Platoon Leader at this time.

More missions were required and after a couple more hours of flying, we were back at Dong Tam, our field standby site. I was a bit tired at the time, so I decided to take a short nap. My co-pilot, crew chief, and flight medic went to get something to eat.

While I was sleeping, I undoubtedly heard something and sat up on the side of my cot. A bit in a daze, I noticed a fairly large rat facing me from the corner of the four-man hooch we were provided. Without any forethought whatsoever, I slowly secured my .38 pistol from the side of my bed, fired, and blew the rat to pieces.

Now, one might not think too much about that, except for the fact that our hooch was sandbagged up to around five feet and located right beside the dental clinic. The pistol shot must have been excessively loud due to the fact that I immediately walked outside and observed a large number of individuals exiting the clinic, some still with white coats and patient vests. I went back inside my hooch, retrieved what was left of the rat by the tail, and I walked back outside saying something like, "Not to worry, all is well." To this day, I have been so thankful that no patient was unduly hurt by my confirmed kill.

About seven days after that field standby, I was scheduled to meet my wife in Hawaii. Since I had immediately started flying missions upon arrival at Dong Tam and was a bit tired, I did not change my bed sheets as we would normally do. The God's honest truth is that I got a case of 'crabs' from the sheets. This aggravated me to no end, knowing that in short period of time, I would be meeting my wife in Hawaii. Now, I didn't know how many cures there were for getting rid of these little pests, but shaving was definitely out of the question. Fingernails and calamine lotion did the trick with a few days to spare. The trip to Hawaii and the time spent with my wife was beautiful and all went very well. As they say, timing is everything.

One other side note about my R&R trip to Hawaii. My friend that was rebuilding the sailboat requested that I buy and bring back the jigging required for the sailboat sails. I was able to accomplish most of that requirement and it's amazing how my small effort enabled me to claim so much construction credit when the subject came up in future conversations about Sea Ducer.

BACK TO VIETNAM

The majority of Dustoff missions in a combat area are exciting in one way or another. Thankfully, most of them go smoothly and without incident. If it were not so, many of our crewmembers would most likely suffer some degree of PTSD (Post Traumatic Stress Disorder). But regardless of the smoothness of the mission, two types seemed to always stick out in my mind. The night hoist and the Navy river patrol boat extraction fit this category.

I will discuss the night hoist mission a bit later, but would like to address the riverboat pickup at this time.

Imagine yourself as a Dustoff pilot or helicopter crewmember attempting to extract a patient or patients from a rapidly moving boat, with radio antennas, on a narrow river, and the possibility of taking enemy fire from either side of that river. Thankfully, on the few occasions that my flight crews and I flew these river pickups, all went well. But the stress factor was always at or near maximum, and our entire crew was always so relieved when such missions were over.

THE TRIAL

Midway through my six-month platoon command time in Vung Tau, I received a call from headquarters at Long Binh that I had been assigned as the Defense Counsel for a couple of our enlisted men in one of our two platoons at that location. The charge was 'possession of marijuana'. I didn't think much about this requirement until I was informed that the two key witnesses for the prosecution were the Company First Sergeant and the Company XO. At the time, the Company XO was the rating officer on my efficiency report.

Now, even though I respected and like both of these individuals, it disturbed me about the setup. I strongly felt that the Defense Counsel should have been someone outside our unit. I was told that the trial was set and it was too late to make any changes. Even though I did not and still do not believe in illegal drug use, I immediately decided that I would do everything that I could to make sure the two accused were found innocent.

Without going into a lot of details, I will simply say that the prosecutor's case was very shaky and the two enlisted men were found innocent. I also can happily say that I don't think the XO, the First Sergeant or my CO ever held my actions against me for doing the best job I could as the defense counsel in the case.

BACK TO FLYING

Our Platoon at Vung Tau was very busy and spread a bit thin. The fact was that on a monthly basis, with four crews on 24-hour duty, (Nui Dat, Van Tau, and two field standbys) we were constantly the leading platoon in both hours flown and patients evacuated. As the Flight Platoon Leader, I was extremely proud of our accomplishments and especially, our safety record, which was flawless. Much of that credit and thanks go to Jack Wofford, our instrument and standardization UH1 and Otter Pilot.

Regardless of how safe one plans to be, peculiar situations can arise that call for special or different actions. As MSC aviators, most of us took a lot of pride in making a difficult situation, such as combat, as nice as possible. I think that we instilled a similar attitude in the Warrant Officers that served with us. As a matter of fact, they weren't that hard to convince.

Along that line, it was customary for the company headquarters at Long Binh to host a periodic party and invite any of our outlying platoon pilots that were off-duty to attend. As strapped as we were, our attendance was usually minimal.

One of our pilots and I were going to be off-duty and we planned to attend one of the upcoming festivities. One of our nurse friends at the 36 Evac hospital heard of the party and said she would like to attend. On the day of the party, the three of us flew over to Lon Binh, about a 45-minute flight. Since the nurse had duty the next morning, we decided we would meet at 0500 hours the next morning in operations in order to get back to Vung Tau in plenty of time for the nurse to get to work.

As it turned out, the other pilot was nowhere to be found the next morning, so the nurse and I took off alone in order to get her back to duty on time. OK, I know what you are thinking. One pilot with a nurse in the co-pilot seat and an emergency arises. How would you explain? Hell, I was thinking the same thing. But remember, she had the duty and chivalry was still alive in those days. All is well, right? Not really.

Flying alone at 2,500 feet, one of the rear sliding door began to open. Undoubtedly that morning, the refueling specialist had not property secured the door. So what were my options? Having the door fly off and striking the tail or main rotor was unacceptable. Having a nurse leave the co-pilot seat and fall out of the aircraft was also unacceptable.

So I gave her a quick lesson on keeping the aircraft straight and level, put the force trim on, and proceeded to leave the cockpit to go and secure the door. By the time I secured the door and got back into my seat, my co-pilot was practicing her right-hand descending turns. Not saying a word, I continued the turn, until we were again headed toward Vung Tau.

I then said, "Good flying, but don't you ever mention this trip to another soul." To this day, I think she complied with my request.

On occasion, I would continue to fly the Otter with Jack. That would occur only on an 'as needed' basis when one of the fixed wing pilots was on R&R, leave status, or grounded.

The radios on the Otter were extremely poor and I can remember being totally out of radio contact with anyone on a number of occasions. This only bothered me during night flying, or over those areas that we had very few, if any, friendly troops.

Another fact about the Otter was that due to its large vertical tail stabilizer, the crosswind landing and takeoff capability could be very critical. In fact, we lost an MSC aviator and a number of other personnel during a crosswind takeoff at the Plantation Air Strip in Long Binh.

On a much lighter note, I remember that Jack had developed a secondary method of getting a message to an intended landing strip when the crosswind was excessive and the radio wasn't working. Yes, we would drop messages attached to small parachutes. Believe it. We did it.

Being Medical Service Corps, with the primary mission of aeromedical evacuation, it is understandable that our personnel always had a very close working relationship with the hospital personnel. The fact was that if our crews were able to get the wounded to the hospital alive, very few either lost limbs or died.

If you have never been involved with medical evacuation and/or direct medical care, two TV series pretty much depicted the way things were in Vietnam. 'Mash' has always been my favorite show and television series and I don't think there is a rerun that I haven't seen. Even though the setting was Korea, it was basically the same as Vietnam. The cold winters of Korea were the main difference.

One other TV series that also exemplified the Vietnam scene was called 'China Beach'. It usually demonstrated the more serious and dramatic aspect of the war and appeared to me to do a good job. 'Mash' was and will always be my favorite. As I have mentioned before, humor and laughter during such serious times served me much better than the sadness.

Another incident that I want to share with you will forever stand out in my mind. Even though I was raised in a Christian environment and made it a practice to always accompany my family to church on Sunday, I did not attend that many services while in Vietnam. My only excuse, and really not a good one, would be that my flight duty usually caused a timing problem.

Well, as it happened, one of my close unit friends was extremely interested in one of the hospital nurses that sang on Sunday mornings in the church choir. He asked me if I would like to accompany him to church the upcoming Sunday. Even though we would both be on flight duty together that Sunday, he assured me that with the chapel being so near our helicopter pad, we would have no problem launching quickly if called. He went on to emphasize his feelings for the aforementioned nurse and that possibly the church attendance might show well for both of us. I agreed to the church visit.

As fate would have it, we were a bit late for the service and when we entered, the choir was in the middle of a song. Now, I don't go so far as to say when the choir saw us enter, they were so surprised that they stopped singing, but I will say that there was a distinct hesitation and noticeable change in their voices. My friend maintained solemn composure but I almost cracked up. So much for our reputations, right? There was quite a bit of follow up to this nurse/pilot relationship, but I think I will wait until I write another book to go into further details.

Continuing on with relationships, another situation that comes to mind had to do with creating a bit of jealously when one felt that things weren't going just right. The 36th Evac hospital had an Officer's Club and most of the time we were considered welcome patrons. It came to my attention that one of our pilots, who was having a bit of a problem with one of the hospital's female nurses, was getting a bit snockered and escorting a number of Vietnamese ladies to the club. Being working girls, they would usually be dressed a bit scantily. Well, the tactic brought too much attention and as the individual's commander, I was asked/told to stop such actions or lose our privileges. The action was stopped and things returned to normal.

All was going well with our Dustoff platoon at Vung Tau. I had been the Flight Platoon Leader for six months. We were continuing to lead the company in missions flown and patients evacuated. Our pilots, crew members, and support personnel were doing a great job and we had incurred no crewmember casualties and were accident free. I was a very proud Flight Platoon Leader with one and one-half years served in Vietnam. I should have expected that things don't stay great forever.

I was on duty this particular night as the AC at Vung Tau. My crew and I had flown two earlier night missions to evacuate some wounded Vietnamese as a result of a mortar attack. It was around 2200 hours when I received a call from Long Binh operations to evacuate an emergency patient from Vung Tau's 36th Evac to Long Binh. I rogered the request and said that my crew and I would be on the way shortly.

Our helicopter was parked on the hospital pad, right next to the hospital emergency room, so I told my co-pilot to start the aircraft and I would check on the patient. Upon entering the emergency room, I noticed a soldier sitting in the waiting area. I proceeded to find the doctor who informed me that the waiting soldier had a small chicken bone lodged in his throat, was in no danger, but that the hospital didn't have the proper instrument to remove the bone.

The doctor suggested that he wait until the next morning to be evacuated. That fit in well with the fact that due to our other flight commitments, we were the only available Dustoff crew in the immediate area. I also mentioned that we might expect some more casualties in the immediate area that night, so I would call Long Binh, explain the situation, and request that they send an aircraft that night or the next morning to evacuate the patient. The doctor agreed. All of this made sense to me since Long Binh had thirteen helicopters and twice the number of crews, plus this was their mission since the patient was not really an emergency.

I called Long Binh and got my friend, Mike Trader, the Operations Officer, on the phone. After explaining the situation, Mike said, "Bill, the patient was called in as an emergency/urgent request, therefore it's your mission."

I said, "It's unreasonable, and not going to happen tonight." I hung up the phone and my crew and I went back to our quarters. It wasn't very long before I received a phone call from LTC Price, the 45th CO and my Commander. He asked why I was refusing an 'urgent' mission.

After listening to my explanation, he said, "Bill, fly the patient to Long Binh now and come in to see me when you arrive."

I won't attempt to describe how upset and pissed off I was, but I really was. Upon arrival at Long Binh that night, I had calmed down a bit, and was intercepted by then XO LTC John Temperilli who suggested that I remain calm while talking with LTC Price. I said, "Fine."

Colonel Price initially emphasized the fact that I should have realized that his Operations Officer, Captain Trader, spoke and acted for the CO and that it was my responsibility to comply with his directions. I elected not to argue the point but stated that due to the circumstances, I strongly felt that Captain Trader was wrong. I went on to say that I was trying to protect and provide the aeromedical services needed in the Vung Tau area.

Regardless of the facts, Colonel Price instructed me to return to Vung Tau, pack my things, and return to Long Binh the next day for reassignment. Even though I was able to maintain my composure, I was crushed. I was being relieved for what I knew was an unfair reason.

Arriving back at Vung Tau and returning to our villa, Jack Wofford was waiting for me. Somehow, the word had already gotten back to Vung Tau and to Jack about what had happened to me and the fact that I would be permanently departing the next morning. The interesting fact was that even though I was still quite upset at Colonel Price, I had accepted what had happened and was prepared to live with the outcome. My friend, Jack, was really upset and wanted to confront Colonel Price personally. I was against that and was able to calm Jack down and assured him that I was OK.

The next morning, I thanked everyone for their support for me as their Flight Platoon Leader, wished them all good luck, and departed to Long Binh for my meeting with Colonel Price. I had consoled myself in the fact that I had gotten my six months of combat command time and that our platoon at Vung Tau had performed extremely well during that period.

At the beginning of our meeting, Colonel Price asked me if I understood his actions and I replied in the affirmative. But I did restate that due to the circumstances, I still felt that Mike Trader, the Operations Officer, had been the one that had made the wrong decision about who should have flown the mission.

As I remember, Colonel Price did not respond to my comment but asked me if I would like to be assigned as the Aviation Staff Officer at the 44th Medical Brigade Headquarters there in Long Binh. Under normal circumstances and having already flown eighteen months of Dustoff aeromedical missions in South Vietnam, I would have jumped at such an opportunity. But this situation was not normal circumstances. The staff officer position would have been great experience for me and might have even enhanced my MSC career.

I hesitated for a few moments and said to Colonel Price, "No, not under these circumstances."

Not only did my answer surprise Colonel Price, but I think it pissed him off a bit. I found out later that he had personally recommended me and had secured the position for me and that there were a number of other MSC aviators that wanted the job.

I further stated to Colonel Price that I appreciated the offer but since I had just been relieved by him, that I wanted a chance to further prove myself in the field environment.

He hesitated for a minute and said, "OK, you will be assigned as Major Fred Belcher's Operations Officer, who has recently taken over the command of the 57th Aeromedical Detachment at Lai Khe." The 4th Platoon, 45th, had recently been replaced by the 57th at Lai Khe.

I said, "That's fine with me."

I later learned that Colonel Price had supported Captain Trader in the previous incident in an effort to teach me a lesson in reference to the 'chain of command' and not in any way to damage my career. That fact was verified since I received an outstanding efficiency report for my command time at Vung Tau.

The main thing that I actually learned reference the incident was that you can teach subordinates valuable lessons without damaging their careers. That fact did mean a lot to me and hopefully meant the same to a number of my younger subordinates along their military paths. I also learned that even though you may be right in a disagreement, it could cost you dearly in the long run.

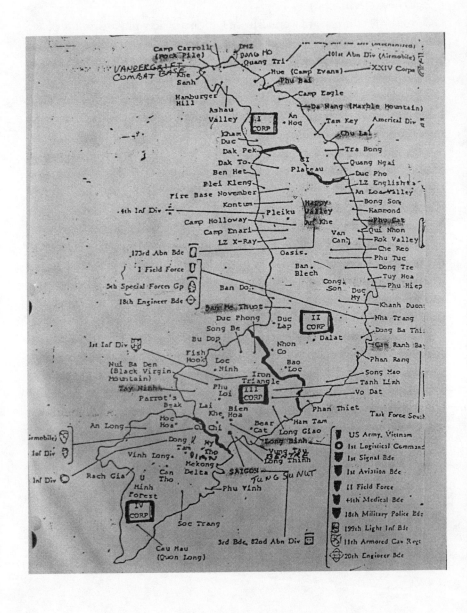

LAI KHE

Upon arrival at Lai Khe and the 57th Med Detachment, I was welcomed by Major Belcher. He had flown his first tour with the 15th Aeromedical Platoon of the 1st Air Calvary and was basically a 'by the book' type commander. I probably needed that and accepted and respected his method of command.

The 57th had a great group of MSC and Warrant Office aviators to include CO Fred Belcher, Pete Langhorne, Pierre Allemand, Gary Stahluth, Tom Hall, Sherman Goodman, Mr. Hammond. Our flight medics, crew chiefs, and support personnel were also outstanding. But I must admit, none of us were as 'straight arrow' as Major Belcher. This fact will become more apparent as you read about the last six months of my second tour in Vietnam.

Our mission was similar to Vung Tau and our Mekong Delta standbys, but the flying was quite a bit more hazardous. We had area support for quite a large part of the III Corp area. The 1st Infantry Division, the 11th Armored Calvary, the 1st Air Calvary, and the 25th Infantry Division were all operating in the area, along with a number of South Vietnamese Units. A lot of combat assault missions were being conducted on a daily basis. We were busy.

Our primary field standby was at Dau Tieng, an area just west of the infamous Michelin Rubber Plantation with both Viet Cong and MVA units throughout the area. Due to the large amounts of jungle and vegetation through our AO (Area of Operation), we were constantly receiving medical evacuation missions that required the use of the hoist. They were always fun, right?

The custom among our pilots was that God forbidding, if you were actually killed or received wounds serious enough to permanently require that you be evacuated out of country, some other pilot had the rights to any of your personal possessions, i.e., stereo, radio, camera, personal trophy weapons, etc.

In line with this custom, my field standby crew on night duty at Dau Tieng received a hoist medevac request for two 1st Infantry soldiers that had suffered gunshot wounds. As it happened, the same request had also gone to our 57th Dustoff Operations at Lai Khe. Since we were airborne first, the first up crew and some other unit personnel were monitoring the radio transmissions at Lai Khe. En route to the hoist site and in contact with both the escort gunships and the ground troops, we received word that the ground troops were on the run and expected to be in a clear area in approximately 20 to 30 minutes. We were asked to orbit to the south and stand by for further instructions.

I confirmed that the two wounded soldiers were in no immediate danger. My co-pilot, Warrant Officer Tom Hall had been in-country on his first tour for a short period of time and we had flown a few missions together. One of the points that I had always emphasized to new pilots was to never get in such a rush that it could result in applying excessive power/collective pitch that could result in a compressor stall and possibly an accident. This point will surface later.

From our orbiting area to the south, we could see that the gunships were firing on some targets in the vicinity of our expected pickup site. After some twenty minutes or so, the ground troop radio operator called and stated that they had the two wounded in a fairly clear area with some three to four foot shrubs and it didn't appear that the hoist would be necessary. He also stated that they would use a strobe light to mark the pickup site.

I rogered the transmission and requested that the patients be ready and that we would be landing shortly. Both the gunships and the ground radio operator rogered my transmission. I told Tom, my co-pilot, that I would fly the helicopter into the landing site and that he would monitor the controls and fly the aircraft out of the site. I told the flight medic and crew chief that I would land the aircraft, if possible, but would get as close to the ground regardless in order to get the two wounded on board.

All was understood and I began the approach to the blinking strobe light. The gunships were flying a figure-eight pattern, low level, just to the south of the pickup site. On short final, I realized that due to the vegetation in the area, I would not be able to land the helicopter but it looked like I could get close enough to the ground in order to load the patients. While hovering and loading the two patients, all hell broke loose with tracers going by the aircraft. I don't actually remember the exact sequence of events, but things went kind of like this.

The enemy firing began just as we were loading the second patient. I remember the gunship team leader screaming over the radio, "Dustoff, you are receiving fire, get the hell out of there."

Right about this time, I took a round bullet into my flight helmet that hit the right top of my skull. The concussion knocked me off of the aircraft controls. During or just before this, I heard our flight medic or our crew chief yell over the radio that we had both patients on board and for us to get the hell out of the area.

As we were exiting the area and I was holding my flight helmet with both hands, I could feel more rounds hitting the aircraft. Upon gaining some sense of composure, I heard Mr. Hall transmitting that I had been shot in the head, all the time ascending the aircraft in a steady, deliberate pace, out of the pickup site. He was performing just as I had previously instructed him to do in such tough situations.

I must admit, it would not have bothered me one bit if he had been just a tad faster. At what I think was about 300 to 400 feet in the air, I looked at all of the instruments and gauges, which were all indicating normal but were a little blurry to my vision. At first, I thought this was a result of perspiration but it was actually blood in my eyes from my scalp wound.

In defense of the ground troops, they had unknowingly walked into an area that had one or more enemy spider traps, hiding some enemy with automatic weapons, our helicopter hovering with a search light and aircraft running lights was just too much temptation, thus the enemy fire.

Upon landing at the hospital pad at Dau Tieng, two doctors met me when I opened my cockpit door to exit the aircraft. I remember saying, "I think I'm OK, take care of the two wounded." I insisted on not removing my flight helmet until lying down on a stretcher in the hospital.

The doctor removed my helmet, felt my scalp and skull and said, "Bill Covington, you are one lucky son of a bitch."

With seven stitches to close my scalp wound, I was as good as new. We had received quite a number of hits to the aircraft. The one that hit me had possibly gone through the hoist pole, entered my flight helmet, then entered my scalp, was ricocheted by my skull and went upward through the greenhouse window above my head. My eldest son, Britt, asked for and has the flight helmet which still has some sprigs of red hair protruding from the exit hole made by the bullet.

Due to a couple of rounds that penetrated one of the main rotor blades, we needed a replacement aircraft. I was informed by Major Belcher, our Commander, that he would be bringing a replacement aircraft and crew from Lai Khe. I stated that I would only need the aircraft, a flight medic, and a crew chief and that Warrant Officer Hall and I would remain on field standby.

Even though I had never been personally wounded until this time, my aircraft had been shot up a number of times and I knew that the best thing for Tom Hall was for him to fly again as soon as possible, preferably that night. As luck would have it, we did fly again that night, with everything going real well.

Our crew returned to Lai Khe a couple of days later and I was told that one of my fellow MSC aviators and a very good friend, upon monitoring our previous night mission where I was wounded, went to our Pilot Roster Board, placed a red 'X' (out of commission) by my name and stated that my Akai tape recorder was now his. What a friend, right?

My first tour Dustoff flying in the II Corps area was quite exciting and I actually received the nickname of 'magnet ass', an endearing term given to those of us who had a knack for attracting excessive enemy fire and actual aircraft damage.

Once we were given some good field standbys in the III Corps and IV Corps areas while stationed at Vieng Tau, our action picked up substantially. But considering all the factors involved. i.e., enemy (NVA and Viet Cong), amount of combat operations and numerous hoist missions, the Lai Khe and Dau Tieng flying proved to be the most hazardous by far.

Our AO (Area of Operation) consisted of the Michelin Rubber Plantation, the Razorbacks, the Mushroom, Tai Ninh Mountain and the HoBo Woods. Day in and day out, you had to expect enemy action on the majority of your missions.

Another fact that I learned, well after my two combat tours in Vietnam, was that the above-mentioned area had the largest and most elaborate number of tunnel systems in all of South Vietnam.

Side note: My eldest son, Britt, and I visited the 'Tunnels of Cu Chi' in the summer of 2008 and saw first-hand just how sophisticated these enemy tunnels really were. These type tunnels often proved to be the answer to our infantrymen's statements of, "They hit us and disappeared, so where did they go?"

ANOTHER LESSON LEARNED

Upon graduating from both fixed and rotary wing flight training, I had always felt that no matter how good you might have thought that you were as a pilot, there was always more that you could learn. This fact was so vividly pointed out to me on another night hoist mission out of Lai Khe and just north of an area we called the 'mushroom'.

This name came from the fact that a river turned in such a way that it formed what closely resembled a mushroom. The hoist mission called for the evacuation of two patients that had received gunshot wounds to their legs.

Now, I want to let you know that the 'pucker factor' can increase quite significantly while sitting in an area loading the wounded. On hoist missions, and especially those performed during darkness, the factor is even higher.

The fact of the matter was, that while sitting on the ground or while hoisting patients, it proved to be the time that you and your crews would take the most fire and actual hits to the aircraft. Statistical data verified this fact. Also, during these hoist missions, not only were you vulnerable to enemy fire, but you were in a dangerous position in case you had any kind of flight emergency, i.e., tail rotor, engine, or transmission failure. OK, so much for painting the scene for hoist missions.

En route to the pickup site, I was informed by the ground troops that they were moving the two patients to a more secure site. I was also told that both patients were stable and in no immediate danger. We were asked to orbit and wait for further instructions. Having flown a previous mission and receiving the call for the hoist mission, I had instructed the crew chief not to add any additional fuel. I felt that we had plenty.

After some time, the ground radio operator called and stated they were ready to commence with the hoist mission. By this time, we had a little less than a half tank of fuel, but plenty to perform the mission and get back to the 2nd surgical hospital at Lai Khe.

Another fact that would impact on this mission was that due to some of our aircraft batteries overheating, we had elected to position them in the nose of the helicopter.

With relatively low fuel, I informed the ground radio operator that we would hoist both patients simultaneously on the hoist forest penetrator. Are you beginning to get the picture?

I did not ask and was not told that both of the wounded were quite large men. They also had some of their combat gear to include their individual weapons strapped to their bodies. We had a lot of the hoist cable out to reach the ground and, as I remember, the trees were quite tall in the area. I was hovering the aircraft from the left seat with my co-pilot monitoring the controls. My co-pilot also had the responsibility to cut the hoist cable if I instructed him to do so. Such an action, for obvious reasons, with a patient or patients being lifted, was always a last resort. Not long after we began to hoist the patients, I noticed that I was rapidly running out of aft cyclic and that the aircraft was beginning to slowly move forward. We continued to hoist and drift forward more rapidly.

My immediate response was to add power and gain altitude in an effort to not further injure the two patients. We were gaining altitude, but the patients were now being dragged through some of the tree branches. Due to the altitude above the ground and the forward speed, I felt that if we cut the cable, the patients' chances of survival were minimal.

Fortunately, we cleared the trees and quickly got the two patients inside the helicopter. Yes, it crossed my mind about the fact that the cable could have gotten stuck in the trees while we were moving forward, but there was no way that we were going to cut the cable and possibly kill both patients.

The next day, I visited both patients in the hospital. They were both doing fine and with smiles on their faces, asked me, "Sir, is that the way all hoist missions are done?"

I said, "No, yours was just a special one."

From that night forward, I have never forgotten just how important weight and balance is when it comes to flying, regardless of the type of aircraft being flown.

LIVING CONDITIONS AND OTHER ACTIVITIES

Living conditions during my two Vietnam tours varied depending on where you were located at the time. I've already noted that during my first tour in the II Corps at Qui Nhon, the 1st Air Calvary at An Khe had it the toughest. Field duty and pup tents were standard for Cav troops – officers and enlisted. We had it much better at Qui Nhon, living in what I would describe as Quonset huts. On occasion, we even had air conditioning, or at least, electric fans. Our field standbys were not as nice, but normally only two to three days at a time. Lai Khe was a similar setup. Our officer shower was enclosed with an emersion heater up top of the roof and had to be manually lighted. The top of the enclosed shower was about eight feet and the barrel holding the water and the emersion heater was even higher. We had a ladder to get on top of the building.

We were all extremely startled one afternoon by a large bang, which came from the shower area. What had happened was that one of our pilots, no name mentioned, was in the process of lighting the emersion heater when the explosion occurred. The blast blew him off the top of the building. When we reached the area, we found our fellow pilot with a blackened face, lodged between three small trees, sitting on the ground.

Looking startled, he asked, "What happened?"

Observing that he appeared to be OK, someone said, "Man, you just blew your own ass off the top of the shower."

To this day, I am amazed that he was not seriously injured. Needless to say, not too many warm showers were taken from that day forward.

WHEN THE BOSS IS AWAY

Being the Detachment Operations Officer and second in command, I was the Acting Commander when Major Belcher took his seven day, out-of-country R&R trip. Remember, I have already written that Major Belcher was both a former 1st Calvary pilot and also could be described as a 'straight arrow' type Commander. He led by example and to a man, we all respected him very much.

When he departed, he simply said, "Bill, you are in charge."

I appreciated that, and especially the fact that he gave no specific directions on how to run the unit during his absence. To this day, I think that he didn't want to give me any specific directions so he wouldn't have to council me upon his return to the unit.

Naturally, I thought this was smart on his part. We had a very good reputation at Lai Khe and extremely dedicated personnel, both officer and enlisted. We also flew what I considered to be one of the toughest combat areas in South Vietnam.

During the week, we had a couple of parties, one each for both our officers and our enlisted men. In fact, I'm sure that some of our officers and enlisted men had some fun that they thought I never knew about. And that was perfectly alright with me.

What happened was that on the third or fourth day of Major Belcher's R&R, I noticed some late hour takeoffs and landings from our Dustoff helipad. The next morning I asked our radio operator about the missions. Sure enough, he reported that we had a couple of night field pickups and a backhaul from the 2nd Surgical there at Lai Khe to Saigon.

Being a bit suspicious and a bit curious. I checked with the 2nd Surgical and was told that they neither received nor transferred any patients the night before. It wasn't too long before the word got out that I had asked about the phantom night missions. A couple of our warrant officers confessed to me that a couple of runs were made to Saigon for morale purposes. I was smart enough not to ask if the missions were of an import or export nature.

I also confirmed that the primary purpose of the flying was on the behalf of some of our enlisted men. That made me feel good. But, I did make it known that no more of these flights were to take place, regardless of who was in command of the unit. To my knowledge, no more took place while I was at Lai Khe.

While on the subject of our Commander, Major Belcher, I would like to relate an incident concerning him that really signifies just how intense some of our flying was.

I was on a field standby at Dau Tieng and needed some backup support from Lai Khe. This was due to the large number of patients that needed to be evacuated and to the severity of their wounds.

Major Belcher was on first up duty at Lai Khe and he and his crew came to give us a hand. After a couple of pickups, I was in the hospital operating room at Dau Tieng when Major Belcher came in from one of his missions. I sensed that he was a bit excited due to the fact that his crew had taken enemy fire and he stated that his crew chief was in the process of checking out the aircraft for damages. He further stated that his co-pilot, crew chief and flight medic were all OK. I happened to look down at his feet and quickly noticed that the heel of his boot had been damaged.

What had happened was that one of the bullets that had entered his aircraft, had gone through his boot and part of his heel. I guess due to the adrenalin rush and all the other excitement, he did not realize that he had actually been wounded. It just goes to show you how such a happening can escape one's notice during a critical and exciting situation.

MOVING ON

I am happy to write that it did not take very long in Vietnam for our Dustoff medevac crews to develop a proud and effective reputation when it came to quickly and safely getting the sick and wounded out of a dangerous situation and on to a medical facility.

Some of my proudest moments came when there was actually no sick or wounded personnel involved. How would that be? I witnessed many acts of bravery, but none more than those of our Long Range Recon Patrols (LRRPs), as they were called.

These teams of seven to ten members were normally dropped into areas of known enemy control with orders to find the enemy, but not to become engaged unless absolutely necessary. Often times, they had no backup and were strictly on their own for a large number of days. On more than one occasion, I was involved with the requirement to evacuate some of their wounded or sick team members.

Upon reaching their location, it was not uncommon for the LRRP team to be on the run. This was apparent due to the fact that they seldom wanted to use smoke or a strobe light (night) to mark their landing site.

Another indicator that the enemy were close on their heels was their tendency to whisper over the radio, instead of transmitting in a normal voice. Dead giveaway, right? We never had to worry about them loading patients too slowly or the entire team boarding the aircraft with any kind of hesitation. As I stated earlier, the team was normally on the run with the enemy very nearby.

On the occasions when I recognized that no team member was actually wounded or appeared sick, I never made that fact a big deal. I always took it as a compliment to our flying ability and attitude to get them out of harm's way before some of them did get wounded or actually killed. As a matter of fact, I always felt that if we didn't rescue them quickly while they were on the run, it would just be a matter of time before someone would be injured. To me, that obviously would have been much worse.

Another night hoist mission that quickly comes to mind was the one where there were three seriously wounded with gunshot wounds. The trees were tall and in order to get close enough to the ground, we had to actually hover below some of the treetops. In such conditions, as pilots you must place great confidence in the crew chief and flight medic giving you very accurate hovering advice so as not to hit the trees with either your main rotor blades and/or especially the tail rotor.

Positioning is really critical while the crew chief and medic are getting the patient(s) into the aircraft. Naturally, during such a mission, and without night vision goggles, you normally have both your landing and search light on. That in itself, makes you feel extremely vulnerable to any enemy in the immediate area.

On this particular mission, all was going well and two of the three patients had been hoisted and loaded into the aircraft. All of a sudden, I heard a loud explosion which actually shook the aircraft. I immediately asked the crew chief, "What was that?"

His response was, "I'm not sure, but whatever it was, it took out the top of one of the large trees just behind the tail of the aircraft."

The ground radio operator immediately said, "Dustoff, the last patient is on the hoist penetrator. Get him up and get out of the area."

After the mission, our entire crew checked the aircraft for damages and found none. We could only surmise that the explosion and tree damage possibly came as a result of the enemy firing an RPG (Rocket Propelled Grenade) at us, either striking the tree prior to reaching the aircraft or missing us and then hitting the tree. Either way, we all felt very fortunate to having not been hit.

The RPG was much more feared by helicopter crews than both the AK 47s and even the .51 caliber enemy machine gun. The aircraft, if no critical component was hit, could survive AK47 and .51 caliber fire, but seldom survived a hit by an RPG. A number of helicopters and crew members were lost in Vietnam as a result of such hits. The movie 'Blackhawk Down' gives the best illustration of such an RPG hit.

WHAT GOES AROUND, COMES AROUND

In life, I have always felt that the old saying of, 'What goes around, comes around' has a way of surfacing from time to time.

Remember the major that I referred to during my first Vietnam tour of duty at Qui Nhon that had some of our unit members building sidewalks and doing other types of special projects? I may have also stated that I always felt that his primary objective was not to greatly improve living or work conditions, but was to provide him an excuse to reduce his personal amount of actually flying Dustoff missions. Back then, mostly due to my extremely short time left on my first tour, I felt his timing and special projects attitude sucked.

It so happened, I got a call from Colonel Price, our commander of the 45th in Long Binh, that this same major, now a LTC, was in-country and was scheduled to take Colonel Price's job when Colonel Price finished his tour.

Now I don't know, and never asked Colonel Price whether or not he knew about my previous altercation with his replacement, but when he stated what he wanted me to do, I kind of thought that he was aware of what had previously happened.

He said to me, "Bill, in an effort to familiarize my replacement with some of our outlying areas, I want to send him to Lai Khe to do some flying."

He went on to say that he wanted him to specifically fly with me and asked if that would be a problem.

I simply said, "Colonel Price, no problem at all, but make sure your replacement is aware of what you have instructed." It was agreed. During our two days of flying together, I was actually disappointed that we actually had very little enemy activity, with the missions being extremely routine. The only one that I actually detected some major concern by Colonel Price's replacement, was a night mission where during landing we disturbed a couple of hooch tin roofs which flew near the aircraft. Neither hit the aircraft and all was well.

Now, I am not a vindictive person by nature, but stories that I heard about this particular individual both after I departed Vietnam on my first tour and also how he commanded the 45th during his second tour, were not commendable. As I said, "What goes around, comes around."

UNEXPECTED AIRSTRIKE

Located on the northeast corner of Lai Khe, well away from the refueling area and very near the 2nd Surgical Hospital, our unit seemed secluded from any rocket or mortar attacks. This was good and allowed for pleasant sleeping conditions and a nice secure feeling,

It should also be noted that I have always been a very sound sleeper. In fact, on some field standbys, I could sleep with 155 MM artillery firing very near my tent. But I had never experienced what happened one night around 2 AM at Lai Khe. I actually felt like I had been knocked out of my bunk, followed by a quick run to what I thought was our underground bunker.

I was crouched in a corner when I actually woke up and realized that I was actually in our weapons/ammo annex. The explosions were the result of a B-52 strike just outside of our outer perimeter. Later on, we could only figure that the strike had been a bit off target. Boy, was it loud and devastating. It's hard to imagine what the NVA and Viet Cong felt during such raids.

GETTING SHOT DOWN

I have stated before how tough and reliable the UH1 is, but my luck ran out during a mission just northwest of Dau Tieng and in an area we referred to as "The Razor Backs'.

The pickup required a steep descent into a confined area, requiring some pivoting of the tail on the way to the ground to avoid any tail or main rotor strikes. At about 60 feet above the ground, we started taking hits recognized by the fact that oil began to cover our windshield. I figured we had taken a hit in some critical area of the aircraft. It was time to exit.

Once above the trees, I observed that the engine oil pressure gauge was approaching zero and the temperature gauge was high and in the red. We had gotten about 1,000 meters from the hostile area and I was now looking for a suitable landing spot.

I called a 'Mayday' and picked a landing site right beside a B-52 crater. A C&C (Command and Control) aircraft answered my Mayday call and said they had me in site. I notified them that I would be landing beside a large bomb crater and requested that my crew and I be picked up immediately.

Just prior to landing, I instructed everyone to secure their weapons and all of their personal gear. My crew chief stated that he would secure the aircraft radio. I also informed the C&C ship that we would be getting into the edge of the bomb crater for security purposes since I had no idea as to whether or not there was any enemy in the immediate area.

Once in the bomb crater, I attempted to get in touch with the C&C ship via my handheld radio. After what seemed like about five minutes, I was able to contact the pilot of the C&C aircraft. He did confirm that he was the AC (Aircraft Commander) of the C&C aircraft and that he had the ground commander of the troops that were in enemy contact in the area where we had received our hits.

He then stated that he had our location and then he began to ask questions about the security of our downed aircraft location, the number of hits that we had taken, whether or not we had any wounded, etc. I informed him that we were a crew of four, that we had secured all of our personal equipment from the aircraft, that no one was wounded, and that we were ready for pickup.

He asked me again about the security of the area and I stated that we were receiving no enemy fire and since we had just recently landed, I had no idea if there were any enemy in the immediate area.

As he began to ask some more questions, I interrupted, swore a couple of times, and said, "Get the hell in here and pick us up, OK?"

He rogered and stated that they would be landing shortly, I understood a bit of reluctance but I also knew that time is a major factor in such situations. I remember that there must have been some excitement with the pilot flying the aircraft since there was quite a bit of rocking back and forth when they landed beside the bomb crater.

All went well and we were taken to Tay Ninh and received another helicopter from Lai Khe. I was later told that the patients had been moved to a more secure area and had been evacuated by another Dustoff aircraft from Lai Khe.

Later on that day, a Chinook with a maintenance crew retrieved our downed helicopter. One of the enemy bullets had gone through the engine oil cooler resulting in our loss of engine oil pressure and the rising engine oil temperature.

I had remembered that I had either read in the aircraft operators manual or had a crew chief tell me that you can safely fly the aircraft under such conditions, but the big question is, for just how long? I chose to land as soon as I felt it was safe. All worked out well since the landing area proved to be a safe one.

JUNGLE SURVIVAL IN THE PHILIPPINES

With about four months to go in my second tour, I received word from Long Binh that they had an open slot for me to attend a jungle survival course in the Philippines and asked if I would be interested in attending. I naturally said that I would certainly like to attend and the following week I departed for Clarke AFB in the Philippines.

Prior to departure, I was instructed to return to Vietnam in ten to twelve days. Since we had been working pretty hard at Lai Khe, I welcomed the opportunity for the break.

Upon arrival at Clark, I was informed that there was both a five or ten day version of the course. I was also told that regardless of which version I chose, I would be remaining in the Philippines for twelve days.

Now, if you remember from my flight training days at Ft. Rucker, escape and evasion training was not one of my favorite pastimes! I immediately stated that the five day course would suit me just fine.

The air force personnel smiled and said, "It's amazing that since we started offering both a short and long course, no one has chosen the latter." We may be Army, but we ain't dumb.

The five day course consisted of two days of classroom instruction at Clark which was very informative and well presented. The six of us were then bused to Subic Bay for the three remaining days of survival in the jungle. It was all very good training. Our instructors were indigenous Filipinos, called Negritos. Their jobs were to both train us and to also act as our enemy during our attempts at escape and evasion.

On one of the jungle exercises, we were given thirty minutes to go and hide in the jungle. We were told that we would be found, so not to worry about getting lost or abandoned. By my watch, I decided that I would spend the initial twenty minutes getting as far away from the starting point as possible. I would spend the remaining ten minutes preparing and getting into my hiding spot. At the twenty minute point, I came up on a sort-of gully well off of one of the main trails. There was also a lot of dead vegetation and leaves. I did what I thought was a very good job of covering my entire body and felt like I could get some sleep before dark.

In no more than ten minutes I heard some noise. A few seconds later, I turned my head and a smiling Negrito with his sheath knife at my throat was crouched beside me. I felt a bit inept about my evasion and escape technique until I returned to camp to find that I was the last to be found.

The exercise was geared to emphasize the fact that unless it is absolutely necessary to leave your aircraft, then don't. Wait for rescue. We were later told that the Negritos were excellent jungle trackers and that they could actually smell Americans at quite a distance.

One of the other facts about the training that was very interesting and informative to me was that if you became hungry enough, practically any type of food will taste good to you. To emphasize this point, we were not given much food while in the jungle for the four days. One of the Negritos came into camp on the second day of training with an extremely large lizard. It appeared to be approximately two and one-half to three feet long.

We were told that the lizard tail was considered a delicacy and that it, plus some rice, would be our meal for the day. We observed as the lizard was killed by one of the Negritos. The tail was then skinned and chopped into small pieces. A medium-sized, hollowed-out bamboo reed would be used to contain the pieces of tail and rice mixture as our meal was cooked over an open fire. Once cooked, we were all given our servings. The rice was tasty but the pieces of lizard tail took a lot of chewing before I felt comfortable about swallowing. Needless to say, lots of water was consumed by all during our lizard and rice feast.

BACK TO CLARK AFB

Upon returning to Clark, we were told that we would be billeted at a motel just outside the main gate of the base. It was a nice motel with an outdoor pool. The rest and relaxation was just great for the remaining days prior to my return to Vietnam.

Prior to going to the Philippines, I had contacted my good friend, Garnett Crask, who was flying U21s out of Tan Son Nhut AFB in Saigon. I had asked him about spending a night or two with him on my return trip to Lai Khe. I called him upon arrival in Saigon and he said he would be out shortly to pick me up.

Upon arrival, Garnett said he had a couple of days off so we could have a nice visit together. When it came time to go, he said, "I'll fly you up to Long Binh and then someone from your unit in Lai Khe can come and pick you up." My other choice to get to Long Binh was a jeep ride. What do you think I chose?

The interesting thing about my U21 flight was that upon arrival and taxiing into the VIP pad at Plantation Army Airfield at Long Binh, we noticed a group of military personnel gathered and seemingly waiting for someone to arrive.

I said to Garnett, "I will be as discreet as possible, so why don't you depart as quickly as possible."

He laughed and said, "OK."

I exited the aircraft and quickly walked by the group of personnel in my civilian attire, returning their salutes. Once inside the operations building, I was told that the group was waiting for some General officer to arrive. I quickly scrounged up a ride to the 45th Air Ambulance Company, my command unit, and departed the area.

Oh yes, my friend Garnett was General Abrams Chief Pilot at this time. What are friends for, right?

BACK TO LAI KHE

Just a few days after returning from the Philippines and getting back to Lai Khe, I was having lunch in the Second Surgical Hospital dining facility when I observed a number of personnel hurriedly depart the facility. I asked what was going on and was told that a wounded patient was being flown into the hospital. I went to see what was going on and expected to see one of our 57th Dustoff aircraft landing.

Instead, I saw an OH6 (small observation helicopter) rapidly approaching the helipad. Knowing that the OH6 aircraft normally flew with a single pilot and observer, I figured that the observer had been wounded. The OH6 crews were normally used as the 'hunters' aspect of what were called 'Hunter-Killer Teams'. The 'killer' portion of the team was normally one or two Cobra Gunships.

As a Dustoff pilot, I have often been told by individuals that had served in Vietnam that our Dustoff/Medevac missions were the most dangerous flying during the war. Some even went on to say that the casualty to missions flown statistics verified that fact. Well, I have always felt differently. Sure, our missions were sometimes dangerous and especially just before landing and sitting on the ground, and during takeoffs from hostile areas. But I always felt that was nothing compared to the danger the OH6 pilots and their observers encountered on their 'Hunter-Killer Missions'.

You see, the OH6 crews mission was to hover close to the ground in order to entice the enemy to open fire, exposing their positions so the Cobra 'killers' could find and engage the enemy. Once exposed, it was only reasonable that the enemy would attempt to shoot down the OH6 crews.

So you see, we in Dustoff always attempted to avoid the enemy. Their mission was to find him, and when they did, they were extremely vulnerable to his fire power. And that was what had happened in this particular case. The OH6 had taken hits with one of the rounds striking and fatally wounding the observer. God rest his soul.

A side note about the units that flew these missions to search for, find, and destroy the enemy. A friend of mine, Gene Boger, was an OH6 pilot in one of these units. He informed me that after awhile, he and his other pilot friends that flew the OH6 part of this mission equation coined the phrase 'Reconnaissance by Exposure'. I'm sure you get the picture.

ONE LAST VISIT TO VUNG TAU

Remember my friend Jack with the heavily damaged sailboat in Vung Tau? We also had flown 'Medicare 278', the fixed wing Otter while I was stationed in Vung Tau.

Well, I received a call from him that he had almost finished all the repairs on the sailboat and he wanted me to come back for the maiden voyage. I told him to give me a call when the boat was seaworthy and I would do my best to be there. The call came about one week later and since I had a couple of days off coming, I said I would be there.

Upon arrival in Vung Tau, Jack picked me up at the helipad at the 36th Evac. On the way to the boneyard (boat repair area), Jack stated that he had arranged for a Chinook crew to sling load the sailboat to the Vung Tau Bay. Knowing Jack like I did, I did not ask for the details of that arrangement. Jack further stated that he already had the boat rigged for sling loading and that the Chinook would be at the boneyard shortly.

Upon arrival at the boneyard and seeing the boat, I could not believe how beautiful it was. Jack had done a great and unbelievable job on reconstruction. With the Chinook arriving, I stayed out of the way while Jack connected the sling hook to the hovering Chinook. As soon as the Chinook lifted the boat, we jumped into the vehicle and headed for the Vung Tau Bay.

Just as we arrived, the Chinook crew was lowering the boat into the water. I immediately felt that the drop was a bit too far out from the shore, but Jack didn't seem surprised. Not long after the sailboat was in the water, it became obvious that the tide was going out and so was the boat.

Jack yelled, "Come on, Cov!" as he dashed into the water and began swimming to try and catch the drifting boat. Feeling that Jack had everything under control and not being the best of an ocean swimmer, I elected to stand watch in order to call rescue, if necessary.

Fortunately, at around the two hundred yard point, Jack caught and boarded the Sea Ducer. The return to the docking point was not a problem for Jack since he had the board equipped with two Mercury 150 motors. And no, I had no idea how or when he secured those motors and I felt it best left that way.

I was able to enjoy a short sailing trip on my visit and later learned that Jack and other certain parties made seventeen other of what he referred to as 'maiden voyages' on the Sea Ducer prior to the completion of his second tour of duty in Vietnam. And, oh yes, the rules for being invited were that you could only sail if you agreed to go topless. And that rule naturally applied to both sexes. True story, just like all the others, and you better believe it.

Just one other memorable incident which occurred prior to my departure from Vung Tau for Lai Khe.

Jack had informed me that he had also invited some of the gunship pilots that had previously flown cover for us that were now stationed in Saigon to come to Vung Tau for a 'maiden voyage'. One of those pilots was none other than the infamous Jim Vance.

If I didn't mention it before, Jim was one of the best, if not the best, gunship pilot that I encountered during my two tours of flying Dustoff in Vietnam. That's the good part about Jim. But he could, on occasion, get a bit loud and boisterous in the social environment. It didn't take me long to learn, that's what helicopter gunship pilots do. Sort of like their jet pilot counterparts in our sister services. You get the picture, right?

To carry on, Jack told me that he had planned to get together that night at the MACV Officer Club with some other pilots around 1830 hours to have a couple of beers and enjoy some of the Filipino entertainers. He asked if I would like to come and I naturally accepted the invitation.

When we arrived, and since the club and entertainment was so popular, a large crowd had already gathered. We joined some of the other pilots at a large, round table and ordered our beers. Upon entry to the club, I had noticed that quite a few high ranking officers from the area were in attendance.

All of a sudden there was quite a commotion and I heard someone yell, "Where the hell is Covington?"

Yes, it was none other than Jim Vance. I stood up from our table just as Jim saw me. He rushed over and grabbed me in a big bear hug. By the time I hugged him back and was trying to tell him about all the 'brass' in attendance, he had jumped up in the middle of the table, dropped his fatigue pants and yelled, "Moon Shot!"

Someone, or a number of 'someones', pulled him off the table. As he sat down, there was a big grin on his face. Thankfully, no one came over to attempt to render any type of punishment. Again, Jim gave another big grin and shouted to one of the waitresses for a pitcher of beer. That was the social Jim Vance in a nutshell. A good time was had by all.

CONCLUSION

A couple of days later, I returned to Lai Khe to complete my second tour in Vietnam. Though I and my fellow unit members had a few close calls in performing our Dustoff flight duties, I am happy to report that we had no one killed or hurt seriously.

For that matter, I am very proud to report that was also the case for my six-month command time while stationed at Vung Tau flying for the Australians and the other friendly forces located in the Mekong Delta.

Were we a bit lucky? Yes, probably so, but I would hasten to add that we were very good at what we were sent to Vietnam to do. That being, to assist in saving lives.

Did we witness death and suffering? Yes. Lots of it.

Were we concerned and compassionate for those that lost their lives or were seriously injured and the family members and friends that also suffered? Most assuredly, we were.

But in my life after Vietnam, I have personally elected to never forget those that have suffered, but to also emphasize those positive and memorable things that occurred.

To take that thought a step forward, in 1980 I was called by Sergeant Egor Johnson who asked if I would assist him in organizing a reunion of some of our pilots, crew members, and other unit members that had served in Vietnam. I immediately volunteered.

We held that first Dustoff Reunion in Atlanta, Georgia in 1980 and have continued to do so on a yearly basis since that time in San Antonio, Texas.

Our 2010 Dustoff reunion will be in February in Panama City, Florida and I will most definitely attend. And you know what? The vast majority of those Vietnam veterans that attend will not want to talk about the hardships and sadness that they may have encountered, but will laugh about and possibly exaggerate some of the things that happened while in Vietnam.

I hope that fact never ceases. I know it won't for me.

Hope to see you in Panama City or San Antonio sometime in the future.

TRIBUTES, ACKNOWLEDGEMENTS, AND OTHER THOUGHTS

Our Fighting Forces ... There are no better or braver in the entire world. For them to have fought, to have endured, and to have won in such a long and difficult battle that was Vietnam, they are forever to be commended. We, as Army Aviators, certainly flew 'Above the Best' soldiers in the world.

U.S. Medical Support and Dedication ... The record speaks for itself. From the initial care of the field medic to a major hospital facility, the life and limb saving is second to none.

Our Dustoff/Medevac Flight Medics, Crew Chiefs, and Gunners ... They were the best and the bravest. We, as pilots, received the most awards and recognition. It should have been the other way around. They were always the most exposed to danger, not us.

Our Sister Services – the Air Force, the Navy, the Marines and the Coast Guard ... We all work best together as a team. We are effective, feared and should be. Our country's strength and safety depends on that fact and we should never forget it.

Helicopter Gunship Support ... Without a doubt, gunship coverage greatly reduced the losses encountered by our Dustoff/Medevac crews, resulting in the safe rescue of many wounded soldiers.

Warrant Officer Aviation Branch ... 75% of our Dustoff/Medevac pilots were Warrant Officers. They served bravely and were the backbone of our lifesaving mission. I salute them all.

Humor and Laughter ... As strange as it may seem, there is a lot of room for humor and laughter in a war zone environment. Maybe the reason is that when so much sadness and danger is all around, one seems to welcome anything that is remotely funny. During my two years in Vietnam, I often felt that humor and laughter were the major factors that contributed to a positive attitude, especially during tough times.

Bravery ... As you have probably heard many times, tough or dangerous situations can bring out the best or worse in a person. I think that is true and I'm very proud to say that the vast majority of such times in Vietnam, I witnessed acts of bravery. On most occasions, it was more of a spontaneous action to accomplish that which needed to be done. To me, the real test of true bravery was when one knew beforehand of the danger to be faced. An infantryman charging an objective under fire or a medic getting to a wounded soldier under such circumstances are two good examples of such bravery. And you know what? Such actions occurred numerous times during my two tours in Vietnam.

Ties With Loved Ones ... You've seen it in the movies and/or you've experienced it first-hand. Nothing is more uplifting than to receive a letter, package, or some other type of communication from a friend or loved one while in a tough situation. And on the other hand, it's just as important to receive a letter for those who are waiting at home for your safe return. So to any and all concerned, don't take such an act lightly if the occasion arises.

Fellow MSC Dustoff Aviators ... I would like to personally thank Colonel Joe Madrano, LTC's Mac McBride, Bill Bentley (deceased), Gib Beltran, Dick Scott, Arlie Price (deceased), Steve Nash, and Jack Wofford for being my friend and helping me in many ways during my two tours in Vietnam. As a young, inexperienced pilot, I needed guidance. All of you, in some way, helped me. As I continued my service career, I tried to do the same for some others. Thanks.

ABOUT THE AUTHOR

William R. Covington was born in Rockingham, North Carolina, the eldest son of Ralph and Juanita Covington, two of the most loving parents that anyone could have. He played and lettered in baseball, football, and basketball at Rockingham High School. Upon graduation, he was awarded a baseball scholarship to Wake Forest University in Winston-Salem, North Carolina. He received his BS degree in Physical Education in 1962 and entered the U.S. Army as a 2nd Lieutenant, Medical Services Corp. While stationed at Ft. Chaffee, Arkansas, 1st Lieutenant Covington applied for and was accepted for Fixed Wing Flight Training at Ft. Rucker, Alabama.

Upon graduation in 1965, 1st Lt. Covington attended and graduated from the Rotary Wing Qualification Course at Ft. Wolters, Texas in May of 1965. After course completion, he was assigned to the 498th Air Ambulance Company, Ft. Sam Houston, Texas as a Medical Evacuation Pilot.

Among other awards, the author received the Silver Star, Distinguished Flying Cross with Three Oak Leaf Clusters, the Purple Heart, Air Medal with 23 Oak Leaf Clusters, Bronze Star, Commendation Medal, Vietnamese Cross of Gallantry, and the Korean Mung Tu for services performed during his two years in the Republic of Vietnam.

After a 25-year career in the U.S. Army, Lieutenant Colonel Covington worked as a Mortgage Banker, a PGA Golf Tour caddy and as an Aviation Manager in the anti-drug program for an American contractor in Bogota, Columbia. He is now retired and resides in Florida.

LaVergne, TN USA
01 September 2010

195469LV00004B/60/P